ير سورة النبأ

TAFSEER SOORATIN-NABA·

(Extracted from the Tafseers of:

at-Tabaree [d. 310 H]

as-Sam`aanee [d. 489 H]

al-Baghawee [d. 516 H]

Ibn Katheer [d. 774 H]

ash-Shawkaanee [d. 1250 H]

and

as-Sa`dee [d. 1376 H]

and additional named reference works).

Compiled and translated by:

Aboo Talhah Daawood ibn Ronald ibn Louis Burbank

Original typesetting by

Umm `Abdillaah Mervet bint Mahboob Ariff

-rahimahallaahu ta`aalaa-

British Library Cataloguing in Publication Data
A catalogue record for this book is available from the British Library.

First Edition: Rama<u>d</u>aan 1430^{AH}/September 2009^{CE}

May Allaah reward all those who participated in the compilation and publication of this book.

Translated by: Daawood ibn Ronald Burbank.

Cover design by: Sa`ad ibn Daawood Burbank.

Published by: <u>Sh</u>ar<u>h</u>us-Sunnah Publishers.

Email: sharhussunnahpublishers@googlemail.com

ISBN: 978-0-9563550-0-3

Table Of Contents:

بسم الله الرّحمن الرّحيم

PREFACE

All praise is for Allaah, the Lord of the whole of the creation, and may He extol and bestow peace and security upon our Prophet Muhammad, and upon his true followers, and upon all of his Companions.

To proceed, then this is the first in a series presenting extracts from the dependable Tafseers, beginning with tafseer (explanation) of the Soorahs of the last section (*juz·*) of the Qur·aan.

The Tafseers from which the extracts are taken are:

(i) 'Jaami`ul-Bayaan', the Tafseer of Imaam Aboo Ja`far Muhammad ibn Jareer at-Tabaree (d. 310 H);

(ii) The Tafseer of Imaam Abul-Muzaffar Mansoor ibn Muhammad as-Sam`aanee (d. 489 H);

(iii) 'Ma`aalimut-Tanzeel', the Tafseer of Imaam Aboo Muhammad al-Husayn ibn Mas`ood al-Baghawee (d. 516 H);

(iv) 'Tafseerul-Qur·aanil-`Azeem', the Tafseer of Imaam Abul-Fidaa· Ismaa`eel ibn Katheer (d. 774 H);

(v) 'Fathul-Qadeer', the Tafseer of Imaam Muhammad ibn `Alee ash-Shawkaanee (d. 1250 H);

(vi) 'Tayseerul-Kareemir-Rahmaan fee Tafseer Kalaamil-Mannaan', the Tafseer of Shaikh `Abdur-Rahmaan ibn Naasir as-Sa`dee (d. 1376 H).

Included along with these are extracts from others works, such as:
-'Tafseer Juz· `Amma' of Shaikh Muhammad ibn Saalih al-`Uthaymeen (d. 1421 H);

- 'Adwaa-ul-Bayaan' of Shaikh Muhammad al-Ameen ash-Shanqeetee (d. 1393 H), and its completion by Shaikh `Atiyyah Muhammad Saalim (d. 1420 H);

-'Zaadul-Maseer' of Abul-Faraj `Abdur-Rahmaan ibn `Alee ibn Muhammad ibn al-Jawzee (d. 597 H);

- the works of Shaikhul-Islaam Ahmad ibn `Abdil-Haleem ibn Taimiyyah (d. 728 H);

- the works of Imaam Muhammad ibn Abee Bakr, Ibn Qayyim al-Jawziyyah (d. 751 H).

The tafseer of each Soorah is followed by: a biography of the compilers of the works of Tafseer; a biography of those from the Salaf whose sayings are quoted in the tafseer; and the chains of narration for the narrations included from the Tafseer of at-Tabaree (along with brief notes about each narrator taken from the works of the scholars of the sciences of criticism of narrators, such as al-Haafiz adh-Dhahabee and al-Haafiz Ibn Hajr al-`Asqalaanee.) An attempt has been made to include only those narrations which at-Tabaree reports with good chains of narration.

The tafseer of each Aayah usually begins with an explanation which contains a wording closest to the actual wording of the Aayah, and this is printed in red.
Double square brackets indicate additions from the translator.

The intent behind this series is to provide an aid to understanding the Book of Allaah -the Most High- in light of its importance in the life of the Muslim, and because of the scarcity of works of Tafseer in the English language.

A sufficient reminder of the need we have to give more time to seeking to understand the Book of Allaah -the Most High- can be derived from two quotes from the book 'al-`Uqoodud-Durriyyah' of Imaam Muhammad ibn Ahmad ibn `Abdil-Haadee (d. 744 H), wherein he describes his teacher Shaikhul-Islaam Ibn Taimiyyah:

"So from that is what he gathered from the sayings of the people of Tafseer, from the Salaf, those who mentioned the chains of narration in their books.

So this would amount to more than thirty volumes. Some of his students have transcribed some of that, and much of it has still not been transcribed by them; and he *-rahimahullaah-* used to say: 'Sometimes, regarding a single Aayah, I refer to about one hundred Tafseers. Then I ask Allaah to grant me understanding of it, and I say: "O One Who taught Aadam and Ibraaheem! Teach me."
[al-`Uqoodud-Durriyyah of Ibn `Abdil-Haadee, p. 29.]

Yet, despite this degree of care and attention, he said whilst in prison:

"Allaah has opened up for me this time, regarding meanings of the Qur·aan and fundamentals of knowledge, such things that many of the scholars would wish to attain, and I have come to regret having used up most of my time on other than the meanings of the Qur·aan." [ibid. p. 27]

So I ask Allaah, the Perfect and Most High, that He makes this something
done purely and sincerely seeking His Face, and that He accepts it,
and that He forgives our shortcomings,
and that He makes it of benefit
to me, my family, and the Muslims,
indeed He is the All-Hearing,
the One Who responds,
and our final call is
that all praise is for
Allaah,
the Lord
of the whole
of the creation.

Written by:
Daawood ibn Ronald Burbank
29th Rajab 1430 H.

INTRODUCTION

All praise is for Allaah. We praise Him, we seek His aid, and we ask for His forgiveness. We seek Allaah's refuge from the evils of our selves and from the evil consequences of our deeds. Whomever Allaah guides then none can misguide him, and whomever He misguides then none can guide him. I testify that none has the right to be worshipped except Allaah, alone, having no partner; and I testify that Muhammad is his Slave and His Messenger.

﴿يَٰٓأَيُّهَا ٱلَّذِينَ ءَامَنُوا۟ ٱتَّقُوا۟ ٱللَّهَ حَقَّ تُقَاتِهِۦ وَلَا تَمُوتُنَّ إِلَّا وَأَنتُم مُّسْلِمُونَ﴾

[*Soorah Aali `Imraan (3): 102*]

[Meaning: O you who believe in Allaah and His Messenger! Fear and be dutiful to Allaah, by obeying Him and avoiding disobedience to Him, as He deserves to be feared (Obey Him and do not disobey Him; give thanks to Him and do not show ingratitude; remember Him and do not forget Him); and do not die except as Muslims: obediently submitting to Him, and worshipping Him alone.]

﴿يَٰٓأَيُّهَا ٱلنَّاسُ ٱتَّقُوا۟ رَبَّكُمُ ٱلَّذِى خَلَقَكُم مِّن نَّفْسٍ وَٰحِدَةٍ وَخَلَقَ مِنْهَا زَوْجَهَا وَبَثَّ مِنْهُمَا رِجَالًا كَثِيرًا
وَنِسَآءً وَٱتَّقُوا۟ ٱللَّهَ ٱلَّذِى تَسَآءَلُونَ بِهِۦ وَٱلْأَرْحَامَ إِنَّ ٱللَّهَ كَانَ عَلَيْكُمْ رَقِيبًا﴾

[*Sooratun-Nisaa· (4): 1*]

[[Meaning: O Mankind! Fear and be dutiful to your Lord, Who alone created you from a single person (Aadam), and from him He created his mate, and from these two He produced many men and women; and fear and be dutiful to Allaah through Whom you ask each other for your rights, and beware of cutting ties of kinship. Allaah is ever a Watcher over you.]]

﴿يَٰٓأَيُّهَا ٱلَّذِينَ ءَامَنُوا۟ ٱتَّقُوا۟ ٱللَّهَ وَقُولُوا۟ قَوْلًا سَدِيدًا يُصْلِحْ لَكُمْ أَعْمَٰلَكُمْ وَيَغْفِرْ لَكُمْ
ذُنُوبَكُمْ وَمَن يُطِعِ ٱللَّهَ وَرَسُولَهُۥ فَقَدْ فَازَ فَوْزًا عَظِيمًا﴾

[*Sooratul-Ahzaab (33): 70-71*]

[[Meaning: O you who believe in Allaah and His Messenger! Fear and be dutiful to Allaah and speak with truth and justice, and He will rectify your deeds for you and forgive your sins; and whoever obeys Allaah and His Messenger has attained tremendous success.]]

To proceed: Then the truest speech is the Book of Allaah -the Most High, and the best way is the way of Muhammad (ﷺ); and the worst of affairs are those things which are new introductions (into the Religion) and every new introduction is an innovation, and every innovation is misguidance, and all misguidance will be in the Fire.

"The *Ummah* (the Islamic nation) has a great and pressing need to understand the Qur·aan, which is the strong Rope of Allaah, and the wise Reminder; one who follows it will not be led astray by desires, and it will not become confused upon the tongues. It does not become dull through repetition, its wonders never cease, and the scholars can never have enough of it. Whoever speaks in accordance with it will speak the truth, whoever acts in accordance with it will be rewarded; whoever judges by it has judged justly, and whoever calls to it then he invites to the straight path. Whichever tyrant abandons it then Allaah will break him, and whoever seeks guidance in other than it then Allaah will misguide him.

He -the Most High- said:

﴿فَإِمَّا يَأْتِيَنَّكُم مِّنِّي هُدًى فَمَنِ اتَّبَعَ هُدَايَ فَلَا يَضِلُّ وَلَا يَشْقَىٰ ۝ وَمَنْ أَعْرَضَ عَن
ذِكْرِي فَإِنَّ لَهُ مَعِيشَةً ضَنكًا وَنَحْشُرُهُ يَوْمَ الْقِيَامَةِ أَعْمَىٰ ۝ قَالَ رَبِّ لِمَ حَشَرْتَنِي
أَعْمَىٰ وَقَدْ كُنتُ بَصِيرًا ۝ قَالَ كَذَٰلِكَ أَتَتْكَ آيَاتُنَا فَنَسِيتَهَا وَكَذَٰلِكَ الْيَوْمَ تُنسَىٰ﴾

[*Soorah TaaHaa (20): 123-126*]

[[Meaning: Then if guidance comes to you from Me, then whoever follows My Guidance shall not go astray and he shall not be wretched; but whoever turns away from My Reminder then he shall have a bleak and constricted life, and on the Day of Resurrection We shall raise him up blind. He will say: 'O my Lord! Why have you raised me up blind when I used to have sight in the world?' He will say: 'Thus it is: Our signs came to you and you turned away from and abandoned them, and so this Day you shall be abandoned.

And He -the Most High- said:

﴿قَدْ جَآءَكُمْ رَسُولُنَا يُبَيِّنُ لَكُمْ كَثِيرًا مِّمَّا كُنتُمْ تُخْفُونَ مِنَ
ٱلْكِتَٰبِ وَيَعْفُوا۟ عَن كَثِيرٍ قَدْ جَآءَكُم مِّنَ ٱللَّهِ نُورٌ وَكِتَٰبٌ
مُّبِينٌ يَهْدِى بِهِ ٱللَّهُ مَنِ ٱتَّبَعَ رِضْوَٰنَهُۥ سُبُلَ ٱلسَّلَٰمِ وَيُخْرِجُهُم
مِّنَ ٱلظُّلُمَٰتِ إِلَى ٱلنُّورِ بِإِذْنِهِۦ وَيَهْدِيهِمْ إِلَىٰ صِرَٰطٍ مُّسْتَقِيمٍ﴾

[*Sooratul-Maa·idah (5): 15-16*]

[[Meaning: There has come to you Our Messenger Mu<u>h</u>ammad (ﷺ), explaining to you much of that which you used to hide from the Scripture, and overlooking much. There has come to you from Allaah a light and a clear Book. By it Allaah guides those who seek His Pleasure to the path which leads to safety and salvation; and He brings them out of darkness into the light, by His Permission, and He guides to the Straight Path.]]

And He -the Most High- said:

﴿الٓر كِتَٰبٌ أَنزَلْنَٰهُ إِلَيْكَ لِتُخْرِجَ ٱلنَّاسَ مِنَ ٱلظُّلُمَٰتِ إِلَى ٱلنُّورِ بِإِذْنِ رَبِّهِمْ
إِلَىٰ صِرَٰطِ ٱلْعَزِيزِ ٱلْحَمِيدِ ٱللَّهِ ٱلَّذِى لَهُۥ مَا فِى ٱلسَّمَٰوَٰتِ وَمَا فِى ٱلْأَرْضِ﴾

[*Soorah Ibraaheem (14): 1-2*]

[[Meaning: *Alif Laam Raa*. This is a book which We have sent down to you, in order that you might lead mankind out of darkness into light, by the permission of their Lord, to the path of the All-Mighty, the One worthy of all praise: Allaah, to Whom belongs everything that is in the heavens and in the earth.]]

And He -the Most High- said:

﴿وَكَذَٰلِكَ أَوْحَيْنَآ إِلَيْكَ رُوحًا مِّنْ أَمْرِنَا ۚ مَا كُنتَ تَدْرِى مَا ٱلْكِتَٰبُ وَلَا ٱلْإِيمَٰنُ وَلَٰكِن جَعَلْنَٰهُ
نُورًا نَّهْدِى بِهِۦ مَن نَّشَآءُ مِنْ عِبَادِنَا ۚ وَإِنَّكَ لَتَهْدِىٓ إِلَىٰ صِرَٰطٍ مُّسْتَقِيمٍ صِرَٰطِ ٱللَّهِ ٱلَّذِى لَهُۥ مَا
فِى ٱلسَّمَٰوَٰتِ وَمَا فِى ٱلْأَرْضِ ۗ أَلَآ إِلَى ٱللَّهِ تَصِيرُ ٱلْأُمُورُ﴾

[*Sooratush-Shooraa (42): 52-53*]

[[Meaning: And likewise We have revealed this Qur·aan to you, as a mercy, by Our Command. You did not know what the Book is, nor what is Faith. But We have made it a light by which We guide whomever We wish from Our servants. And you certainly guide Our servants towards the Straight Path: the Path of Allaah, to Whom belongs whatever is in the heavens and whatever is in the earth. Certainly all affairs shall return to Allaah for judgement.]]

... It is binding that a person should know that the Prophet (ﷺ) explained the meaning of the Qur·aan to his Companions, just as he made clear to them its Words.

So His Saying -He the Most High:

﴿وَأَنزَلْنَآ إِلَيْكَ ٱلذِّكْرَ لِتُبَيِّنَ لِلنَّاسِ مَا نُزِّلَ إِلَيْهِمْ﴾

[*Sooratun-Nahl (16): 44*]

[[Meaning: And We sent down this Qur·aan to you, O Muhammad (ﷺ), as a reminder to them, so that you should then explain clearly to the people what has been sent down to them] [1] includes both this and that [i.e. the Words and the meaning.]]

---

[1] as-Suyootee quoted in his 'Miftaahul-Jannah fil-I`tisaam bis-Sunnah' (p. 58): "Ibn Mas`ood said, as reported by Ibn Abee Haatim: 'There is nothing except that it has been made clear to us in the Qur·aan, however our understanding falls short of reaching it, so therefore He -the Most High- said:

﴿وَأَنزَلْنَآ إِلَيْكَ ٱلذِّكْرَ لِتُبَيِّنَ لِلنَّاسِ مَا نُزِّلَ إِلَيْهِمْ﴾ [*Sooratun-Nahl (16): 44*] [[Meaning: So that you, O Muhammad (ﷺ), should then explain clearly to the people what has been sent down to them]].'

And Aboo `Abdir-Rahmaan as-Sulamee said: 'Those who taught us the recitation of the Qur·aan, such as `Uthmaan ibn `Affaan, `Abdullah ibn Mas`ood, and others, when they had learned ten Aayahs from the Prophet (ﷺ), would not go beyond them until they had learned what they contained from knowledge and action. They said: So we learned the Qur·aan, and knowledge, and action, together.'[2]

Therefore they used to remain for a period of time learning a Soorah, and Anas said: "When a man had learned [Soorah] *al-Baqarah* and [Soorah] *Aali `Imraan* he attained stature in our eyes"[3], and Ibn `Umar took some years to learn *al-Baqarah*, it is said that it was eight years; Maalik mentioned it.[4]

And that was because Allaah -the Most High- has said:

﴿ كِتَـٰبٌ أَنزَلْنَـٰهُ إِلَيْكَ مُبَـٰرَكٌ لِّيَدَّبَّرُوٓا۟ ءَايَـٰتِهِۦ ﴾ [*Soorah Saad (38): 29*]

[[Meaning: This Qur·aan is a Book which We have sent down to you, full of blessings, so that they may reflect upon its Aayahs.]]

And He said: ﴿ أَفَلَا يَتَدَبَّرُونَ ٱلْقُرْءَانَ ﴾ [*Sooratun-Nisaa· (4): 82*]

[[Meaning: Will they not carefully reflect upon the Qur·aan?]]

And He said: ﴿ أَفَلَمْ يَدَّبَّرُوا۟ ٱلْقَوْلَ ﴾ [*Sooratul-Mu·minoon (23): 68*]

[[Meaning: Have they not reflected upon the Qur·aan?]]

---

[2] as-Suyootee quoted in his 'Miftaahul-Jannah fil-I`tisaam bis-Sunnah' (2/437): "at-Tabaree reported it in his 'Tafseer' (1/60), and as-Samarqandee in his 'Tafseer' (1/71) and Ibn Sa`d in 'at-Tabaqaat' (6/172), and Ibn Abee Shaybah in 'al-Musannaf':..6/117, and its chain of narration contains `Ataa· ibn as-Saa·ib:*Sadooq* (truthful), whose memory deteriorated; however the narrator from him is Hammaad ibn Zayd, as occurs in 'as-Siyar' (4/269), and his narrations from him are good..."

[3] Reported by Imaam Ahmad (3/120). Shu`ayb al-Arnawoot said in his checking of the 'Musnad' (no. 12236): "Its chain of narration is '*saheeh*' to the standard of the two Shaikhs."

[4] Imaam Maalik stated in his 'Muwatta·' (1/205) that it had reached him (*balaaghan*) that `Abdullaah ibn `Umar had remained for eight years learning Sooratul-Baqarah.

And carefully reflecting upon speech is not possible without understanding its meaning.

Likewise He -the Most High- said:

﴿ إِنَّآ أَنزَلْنَٰهُ قُرْءَٰنًا عَرَبِيًّا لَّعَلَّكُمْ تَعْقِلُونَ ﴾ [*Soorah Yoosuf (12): 2*]

[[Meaning: We have sent it down as an Arabic Qur·aan, in order that you may comprehend its meaning]], and comprehending speech includes understanding it.

It is also known that what is intended from all speech is that its meaning be understood, not just its wording, so the Qur·aan has more right to that; and also the normal behaviour of the people prevents them from reading a book in any field of knowledge, be it medicine or mathematics, and then not seeking necessary explanation of it. So how about the Speech of Allaah, which is their essential safeguard, and through which they are to attain salvation and bliss, and by means of which their Religion and their worldly lives are correctly established?!

This is why disagreement amongst the Companions with regard to the tafseer of the Qur·aan was extremely rare; and even though it occurred more amongst the Taabi`een (the Successors of the Companions) than it did amongst the Companions, then still it was little in comparison to what occurred with those who came after them. So the more excellent a time was, then the greater the unity, the harmony, the knowledge, and the clarity of understanding was in it.

So from the Taabi`een there were those who learned the whole tafseer from the Companions, just as Mujaahid said: "I went through the whole *mus-haf* with Ibn `Abbaas, stopping him at every Aayah and asking him about it."[5]

---

[5] Fawwaaz Ahmad Zumarlee said in his checking of as-Suyootee's 'al-Itqaan' (2/473): "It was reported in 'al-Hilyah' (3/280)..; and it was reported by at-Tabaree in his 'Tafseer'(1/65), and Aboo Nu`aym in 'al-Hilyah' (3/279-280); and its chain of narration contains Muhammad ibn Ishaaq who narrated it with both of them with *`an`anah* (without stating that he had heard it directly from the narrator before him); however it has another chain of narration which supports it, since it was also reported by al-Qaasim ibn Sallaam in 'Fadaa·ilul-Qur·aan' (p. 216), and by Ahmad in 'al-Fadaa·il' (no. 1866), and its chain of narration contains Ibn Abee Najeeh, who reported a great amount from Mujaahid; but he

Therefore ath-Thawree said: "If tafseer comes to you from Mujaahid, then it will suffice you."[6]

Therefore his tafseer was relied upon by ash-Shaafi`ee, al-Bukhaaree, and others from the people of knowledge; and likewise Imaam Ahmad, and others who wrote works of tafseer, would repeatedly quote chains of narration from Mujaahid, more so than from others besides him. So what is intended is that the Taabi`een took the tafseer from the Companions, just as they took knowledge of the Sunnah from them....

As for Tafseer, then the people who were most knowledgeable about it were the people of Makkah, since they were the students of Ibn `Abbaas, such as: Mujaahid, `Ataa· ibn Abee Rabaah, `Ikrimah-the freed slave of Ibn `Abbaas, and others from the students of Ibn `Abbaas, such as: Taawoos, Abush-Sha`thaa·, Sa`eed ibn Jubayr, and their like.

Likewise the people of al-Koofah, from the students of Ibn Mas`ood, and they had distinction in some of that over others; and the scholars of tafseer from the people of al-Madeenah, such as Zayd ibn Aslam - whom Maalik took tafseer from, and likewise his [i.e. Zayd's] son `Abdur-Rahmaan took it from him (also), and `Abdullaah ibn Wahb took it from `Abdur-Rahmaan...

And in summary, whoever turns away from the positions of the Companions and the Taabi`een, and their tafseer, in favour of something contrary to that, then he is in error in doing that, indeed he is an innovator; unless if he is performing legitimate ijtihaad, in which case his error is forgiven...

So if someone were to say: 'What is the best approach with regard to Tafseer?' Then the answer is that the most correct approach is to explain the Qur·aan with the Qur·aan. So what has been left unspecified at one place will be explained at another place, and what is mentioned briefly at one point will be detailed elsewhere...

And if you become unable to do that, then take hold of the Sunnah, for the Sunnah explains and clarifies the Qur·aan..., and when we do not find the

---

would narrate from him things that he had not heard directly from him. Refer to 'Tabaqaatul-Mudalliseen' (p. 9)."

[6] Reported by at-Tabaree in his 'Tafseer' (1/65).

tafseer in the Qur·aan, nor in the Sunnah, then we refer back for that to the sayings of the Companions, for they knew best about it because of what they actually witnessed relating to the Qur·aan, and because of the circumstances particular to them, and because of their complete understanding, their correct knowledge, and their righteous deeds...

And if you do not find the tafseer in the Qur·aan, nor in the Sunnah, nor do you find it from the Companions, then many of the imaams refer back in that case to the statements of the Taabi`een, such as Mujaahid ibn Jabr... and such as Sa`eed ibn Jubayr, `Ikrimah-the freed slave of Ibn `Abbaas, `Ataa· ibn Abee Rabaah, al-Hasan al-Basree, Masrooq ibn al-Ajda`, Sa`eed ibn al-Musayyib, Abul-`Aaliyah, ar-Rabee` ibn Anas, Qataadah, ad-Dahhaak ibn Muzaahim, and others from the Taabi`een, and those who succeeded them, and those who came after them.

So their sayings are mentioned with regard to an Aayah, and the wordings which they used may differ, and so one who has no knowledge may think that they are disagreements, when this is not actually the case. So some of them may refer to something by mentioning that which it necessitates, or by mentioning that which corresponds to it, and some of them may state the actual thing itself; and all of these actually have the same meaning, and this occurs in many places, so let the discerning person be alert to this; and Allaah is the One Who guides."[7]

[7] Taken from 'Muqaddimah fee Usoolit-Tafseer' (pp. 43-47, 71-72, 91, 93-94, 96, 100-101) of Shaikhul-Islaam Ibn Taimiyyah; and it occurs in 'Majmoo`ul-Fataawaa' (13/329-375).

TRANSLITERATION GUIDE:

a	-	(َ)	z	-	ز
i	-	(ِ)	s	-	س
u	-	(ُ)	s̲h̲	-	ش
aa	-	(َا)	s̲	-	ص
oo	-	(ُو)	d̲	-	ض
ee	-	(ِي)	t̲	-	ط
ay/ai	-	(َي)	z̲	-	ظ
aw/au	-	(َو)	`	-	ع
·	-	ء	g̲h̲	-	غ
b	-	ب	f	-	ف
t	-	ت	q	-	ق
t̲h̲	-	ث	k	-	ك
j	-	ج	l	-	ل
h̲	-	ح	m	-	م
k̲h̲	-	خ	n	-	ن
d	-	د	h	-	ه
d̲h̲	-	ذ	w	-	و
r	-	ر	y	-	ي

SOORATUN-NABA·

AT-TIRMIDHEE reported in his Sunan: Book of the Tafseer of the Qur·aan: Chapter 57… (no. 3297):

"Aboo Kurayb narrated to us: Mu`aawiyah ibn Hishaam narrated to us: from Shaybaan: from Aboo Ishaaq: from `Ikrimah: from Ibn `Abbaas who said: Aboo Bakr- *radiyallaahu `anhu-* said:

"O Messenger of Allaah, your hair has started to turn grey!"

He said: **<< I have been turned grey-haired by *Hood*, *al-Waaqi`ah*, *al-Mursalaat*, and** ﴿عَمَّ يَتَسَآءَلُونَ﴾ [*Sooratun-Naba·*] **and** ﴿إِذَا ٱلشَّمْسُ كُوِّرَتْ﴾ [*Sooratut-Takweer*]. >>

[Saheeh: 'Saheeh Sunanit-Tirmidhee' (3497) and 'as-Saheehah' (no. 955) of Shaikh al-Albaanee *-rahimahullaah*]

بسـم الله الرّحمن الرّحيـم

SOORATUN-NABA· (78)

(Sent down in the Makkan period)

نَبَأٌ

news, information

﴿ عَمَّ يَتَسَآءَلُونَ ﴾ (1)

*AT-TABAREE: "He -the Most High- says: 'About what are those Mushrikoon (those who worship others along with Allaah) (who disbelieve) in Allaah and His Messenger, from Quraish, asking one another, O Muhammad?'

And this was said to him (ﷺ) because the Quraish, as is mentioned about them, began arguing and disputing with regard to that which Allaah's Messenger (ﷺ) called them to: that they should affirm his Prophethood, and believe in that which he came with from Allaah, and that they should believe in the Resurrection. So Allaah said to His Prophet: What are those people asking one another about and disputing about?..."

عَمَّا = عَنْ مَا

about what?

يَتَسَاءَلُونَ

they ask one another

VI root of:

(he asked) سَأَلَ

*AL-BAGHAWEE: "﴿ عَمَّ ﴾ is in origin (عَنْ مَا) [[about what?]]...

﴿ يَتَسَآءَلُونَ ﴾ meaning: What are those Mushrikoon asking one another about? This was because the Prophet (ﷺ) when he called them to Tawheed (making all of their worship purely for Allaah alone), and informed them of the Resurrection after death, and recited the Qur·aan, they started questioning one another and saying: 'What has Muhammad (ﷺ) come with?' az-Zajjaaj* said: "The wording is in the form of a question, but its meaning is to emphasise the importance of the affair."

*az-Zajjaaj, Aboo Ishaaq Ibraaheem ibn Muhammad ibn as-Sariyy, al-Baghdaadee. The scholar of Arabic grammar of his time, author of 'Ma`aaniyyul-Qur·aan', d. 311 H.

*IBN KATHEER: "He -the Most High- says, rebuking the Mushrikoon for their questioning each other about the Day of

Resurrection, which they denied would occur: ﴿عَمَّ يَتَسَآءَلُونَ﴾ [[About what are they asking one another?!]]"

﴿عَنِ ٱلنَّبَإِ ٱلْعَظِيمِ﴾ (2)

عَنْ
About, concerning

نَبَأٌ
news

عَظِيمٌ
very great, tremendous

*These numbers refer to the chains of narration for the reports: see Appendix 2

*AT-TABAREE: "Then Allaah informed His Prophet (ﷺ) what it was they were asking one another about, so He said: 'They are asking one another about the tremendous news.'

Then the people of interpretation differed concerning what is meant by the 'tremendous news'.

So some of them said: It means the Qur·aan.

...Mujaahid[1][2] said, concerning the Saying of Allaah:

﴿عَنِ ٱلنَّبَإِ ٱلْعَظِيمِ﴾: "The Qur·aan."

*Others said: It means the Resurrection.

* ...Qataadah[1] said: "It is the Resurrection after death."

*...Ibn Zayd[1] said: "The Day of Resurrection…"."

*AL-BAGHAWEE: "Then He mentioned what it was which they questioned one another about, saying: ﴿عَنِ ٱلنَّبَإِ ٱلْعَظِيمِ﴾ : [[About the tremendous news]]: Mujaahid and the majority said: "It is the Qur·aan," and the evidence for that is His Saying:

﴿قُلْ هُوَ نَبَؤٌا۟ عَظِيمٌ﴾
[*Soorah Saad (38): 67*]

[[Meaning: Say: This Qur·aan is tremendous news]];

and Qataadah said: It is the Resurrection."

*IBN KATHEER: "Meaning: What are they questioning each other about, with regard to the Resurrection? And it is the 'tremendous news', meaning news which is terrible, awful and overwhelming. Qataadah and Ibn Zayd said: 'The tremendous news' is the resurrection after death, whereas Mujaahid said: It is the Qur·aan, but what is most apparent is the first saying."

*Shaikh `Atiyyah Muhammad Saalim said, in his completion of ash-Shanqeetee's 'Adwaa· ul-Bayaan':

"So that which they questioned each other about was left unclarified to begin with. Then it was clarified to be their questioning each other about the tremendous news. However it still remains to clarify what this tremendous news actually is.

So it has been said: It is the Messenger (ﷺ), with regard to his being sent to them as a Messenger;

And it is said: It is the Qur·aan which was sent down to him, and with which he called them;

And it is said: It is the Resurrection after death.

So Ibn Jareer [at-Tabaree] preferred the permissibility of its covering all of these things, and there being no contradiction between them.

So the reality is that they are all inherently connected, since whoever denies one of them will deny all of them: and whoever truly affirms one of them will affirm them all; and whoever disputes about one of them will dispute about all of them.

However the context refers to the tremendous news (*an-Naba·*), and this is in the singular form, so what is specifically referred to here?

Ibn Katheer and al-Qurtubee said: Those who say that it is the Qur·aan say so because of the evidence of His Saying:

﴿ قُلْ هُوَ نَبَؤٌا۟ عَظِيمٌ أَنتُمْ عَنْهُ مُعْرِضُونَ ﴾

[*Soorah Saad (38): 67-68*]

[[Meaning: Say: This Qur·aan is tremendous news, from which you turn away]]; and those who say that it is the Resurrection say so because of the evidence of the Aayah which comes afterwards:

﴿إِنَّ يَوْمَ ٱلْفَصْلِ كَانَ مِيقَـٰتًا﴾

[*Soorah Naba· (78): 17*]

[[Meaning: The Day when Allaah will judge the creation is an appointed time for the sentence which Allaah will apply to the deniers of the Resurrection]].

So what is apparent, and Allaah -the Most High- knows best, is that what is most clearly supported by evidence is that it is the Day of Resurrection and the return to life, since it is followed by all of the evidences and clear proofs for the Resurrection. It is also followed by a direct statement about the day when Allaah will judge between the creation (i.e. *Aayah 17*).

Then as for the proofs for the Resurrection, then they are four, and they are well-known:

(i) the creation of the earth and the heavens [[*Aayahs 6 and 7, and Aayahs 12 and 13*]];

(ii) the bringing to life of the earth, with the growth of plants [[*Aayahs 14-16*]];

(iii) the original creation of man from non-existence [[*Aayah 8*]]; and

(iv) revival of the dead in this world [[*Aayah 9*: where sleep, which is a cessation of movement and a 'lesser death', is mentioned]]…"

﴿ ٱلَّذِى هُمْ فِيهِ مُخْتَلِفُونَ ﴾ (3)

*AT-TABAREE: "He -the Most High- says: About which they disagreed and became two groups: one group believing and the other group disbelieving."

*...Qataadah[1] said: "The people divided into two regarding it: Believers and Disbelievers. But as for death, then all of them believed in it since they witnessed it; however they disagreed about the Resurrection after death."

*...Ibn Zayd[1] said: "They said: 'This day in which you claim that we and our forefathers will be brought to life!' He said: So they disagreed concerning it, not believing in it. So Allaah said: Rather it is tremendous news which you are turning away from: the Day of Resurrection which they did not believe in."

*AL-BAGHAWEE: "Some believing and some disbelieving."

*AS-SA`DEE: "Meaning: About the tremendous news which they have long disputed about, and about which their disagreement has become widespread; such that they deny it and hold it to be something very far-fetched. However, it is the news which is such that there can be no doubt about; but those who deny the meeting with their Lord do not believe, even if every sign were to come to them, until they will actually see the painful punishment."

الَّذِي
which

هُمْ
they

فِيهِ
about it

مُخْتَلِفُونَ
disagreeing

from إِخْتَلَفَ
(he disagreed)

VIII root of:
(خَلَفَ)

﴿ كَلَّا سَيَعْلَمُونَ ﴾ (4)

كَلاَّ
but no!
سَيَعْلَمُونَ

*AT-TABAREE: “He -the Most High- says: No, the affair is not as those Mushrikoon claim: those who deny that Allaah will raise them to life after their deaths. So He -the Majestic in praise- threatened them for this saying of theirs.

they will come to know
from عَلِمَ (he knew)

So He said: ﴿ سَيَعْلَمُونَ ﴾ that those Disbelievers who deny what Allaah has threatened His enemies with, will come to know what Allaah is going to do with them on the Day of Resurrection.”

*AL-BAGHAWEE: “﴿ كَلَّا ﴾ is a repudiation. He says: They will come to know the result of their denial when the affairs are uncovered.”

*IBN KATHEER: “This is a severe threat and an emphatic warning.”

﴿ ثُمَّ كَلَّا سَيَعْلَمُونَ ﴾ (5)

ثُمَّ
then

*AT-TABAREE: “Then He emphasised the threat by repeating it, saying: the affair is not as they claim: that Allaah will not restore them to life after their deaths, and that He will not punish them for disbelieving in Him. They will know that the true saying is other than what they say, when they meet Allaah: when they go to face the evil deeds which they have put forward.”

*AL-BAGHAWEE: “This is a threat for them, following on from another threat. ad-Dahhaak said: “﴿ كَلَّا سَيَعْلَمُونَ ﴾ means: the Disbelievers, ﴿ ثُمَّ كَلَّا سَيَعْلَمُونَ ﴾ means: the Believers.”

Then He mentioned those things which He has made, so that they should know His Tawheed (His sole right to all worship). So He said: … [*next Aayah*].”

*AS-SAM`AANEE: “What is apparent is that both of the Aayahs refer to the Disbelievers.”

*AS-SA`DEE: “Meaning: They will know, when the punishment comes upon them, that which they used to deny: when they are summoned to enter the Fire of Hell, and it is said to them:

﴿ هَٰذِهِ ٱلنَّارُ ٱلَّتِي كُنتُم بِهَا تُكَذِّبُونَ ﴾

[*Sooratut-Toor (52): 14*]

[[Meaning: This is the Fire which you used to deny.]]”

*Shaikh `Atiyyah Muhammad Saalim said, in his completion of ash-Shanqeetee’s ‘Adwaa· ul-Bayaan’:

“He does not make clear here whether they already knew or not. However He then mentions the Aayahs showing His amazing Power and Ability to resurrect them after death, which gives an indication of that which they were disagreeing about. So it is as if it is being said to them: if you are disagreeing about affirmation or denial of this Resurrection, then here are His Signs and clear proofs: so take admonition from them and derive a lesson from the analogy with them. So the One Who has the Power and Ability to create these things is able to create their like.

However, true and certain knowledge will come about when they actually see that: they have not attained that yet, as indicated by the (سَ) which indicates something in the future. So just as occurs in *Sooratut-Takaathur* [*(102): 1-7*]

﴿ أَلْهَىٰكُمُ ٱلتَّكَاثُرُ حَتَّىٰ زُرْتُمُ ٱلْمَقَابِرَ كَلَّا سَوْفَ تَعْلَمُونَ ثُمَّ كَلَّا سَوْفَ تَعْلَمُونَ كَلَّا لَوْ تَعْلَمُونَ عِلْمَ ٱلْيَقِينِ لَتَرَوُنَّ ٱلْجَحِيمَ ثُمَّ لَتَرَوُنَّهَا عَيْنَ ٱلْيَقِينِ ﴾

[[Meaning: Mutual rivalry in amassing worldly wealth has diverted you from obedience to your Lord, until you come to occupy your graves. But you will certainly come to know the truth that you should not have been diverted by that. Then you will certainly come to know the truth. So if only you knew for certain that Allaah will indeed resurrect you then you would not let that divert you. So you will certainly see the Fire of Hell, on the Day of Resurrection. Then you will certainly see it with your eyes.]]
So this is what they will come to know on the Day when Allaah passes judgement, as is mentioned in the context:

﴿ إِنَّ يَوْمَ ٱلْفَصْلِ كَانَ مِيقَـٰتًا ﴾

[*Soorah Naba· (78): 17)*]

[[Meaning: The Day when Allaah will pass judgement between the creation is an appointed time.]]"

﴿ أَلَمْ نَجْعَلِ ٱلْأَرْضَ مِهَـٰدًا ﴾ **(6)**

أَ
[introduces a question]
لَمْ
did not
نَجْعَلُ
We make, We place...

*AS-SA`DEE: "Meaning: Have We not favoured you with tremendous favours, so We made (the earth) a place spread out, flattened and prepared for you and for your benefit: for agriculture, habitation and for roads."

*AT-TABAREE: "Allaah -the Most High- says, recounting His favours to those Mushriks (those who worship others along with Allaah), and His fine treatment of them, and their ingratitude for His favours upon them; and threatening them with what He has prepared for them when they come to Him: the different forms of punishment and painful torment. So He said to them: ﴿ أَلَمْ نَجْعَلِ ٱلْأَرْضَ مِهَـٰدًا ﴾ ...”

*IBN KATHEER: “Then He -the Exalted and Most High- began making clear His tremendous Power to create amazing and astonishing things, which prove that He has the ability to do whatever He wishes concerning the affair of the Resurrection and anything else besides. So He said: ﴿ أَلَمْ نَجْعَلِ ٱلْأَرْضَ مِهَـٰدًا ﴾ meaning: [[have We not made the earth]] spread out for the creation, manageable for them, settled, stable and firm.”

*ASH-SHAWKAANEE: “Then He -the Perfect- mentioned His amazing creation and His tremendous Power, so that they should recognise His *Tawheed* (His Sole right to all worship) and truly believe in what His Messenger came with. So He said:

﴿ أَلَمْ نَجْعَلِ ٱلْأَرْضَ مِهَـٰدًا وَٱلْجِبَالَ أَوْتَادًا ﴾ [*Aayahs 6 and 7*]

meaning: Our Power and Ability to do these things which are mentioned is something greater than Our Ability to restore to life by resurrecting; and the ﴿ مِهاد ﴾ is a place where one lies down, a bed; just as He said:

﴿ ٱلَّذِى جَعَلَ لَكُمُ ٱلْأَرْضَ فِرَٰشًا ﴾

[*Sooratul-Baqarah (2): 22*]

[[Meaning: He Who made the earth a resting place for you.]]

The majority recite it ﴿ مِهاد ﴾, whereas Mujaahid, `Eesaa and some of the reciters of Koofah recited it ﴿ مَهْدًا ﴾ and the meaning is: that it is like the cradle of a baby, which he is put to sleep upon.”

جَعَلَ from

الأَرْضُ the earth

مِهَادٌ a cradle, a resting place, flat land

people to put a stop to harmful activity, and to bring about beneficial relaxation for them."

❖

(10) ﴿ وَجَعَلْنَا ٱلَّيْلَ لِبَاسًا ﴾

لَيْلٌ
night

لِبَاسٌ
a garment, a covering

*AT-TABAREE: "He -the Most High- says: And We have made the night a covering for you, covering you with its darkness, and covering you just as a garment covers the one who wears it, in order that you may rest from the work which you do during the day."

*IBN KATHEER: "Meaning: Covering the people with its darkness and blackness."

❖

(11) ﴿ وَجَعَلْنَا ٱلنَّهَارَ مَعَاشًا ﴾

نَهَارٌ
day-time

مَعَاشٌ
livelihood

*AT-TABAREE: "He says: And We made the day bright for you so that you may go about to seek your livelihood, and so that you may act in it for attainment of your worldly benefits, and so that you may seek Allaah's bounty therein."

*...Mujaahid [1][9] said: "So that they may seek Allaah's bounty in it."

*IBN KATHEER: "Meaning: We have made it shining, brilliant, and bright; so that the people are able to act, and to come and go for their livelihoods: to earn a living, carry out trade and so on."

❖

﴿ وَبَنَيْنَا فَوْقَكُمْ سَبْعًا شِدَادًا ﴾ (12)

*AT-TABAREE: "He -the Most High- says: And We have raised as a ceiling above you… So He called the ceiling a '*binaa*'' (a vault/raised structure), since the Arabs used to call the roof of a house, which is its highest part, a '*binaa*''. So He addressed them in their language, since the Revelation came down in their language; and He said: ﴿ سَبْعًا شِدَادًا ﴾ [[Seven strong heavens]]: since they are firm and strongly made. They do not contain any gaps or cracks, nor are they worn away by the passage of nights and days."

*AL-BAGHAWEE: "Meaning: Seven heavens."

*IBN KATHEER: "Meaning: The seven heavens with their vast expanse and height, and their firmness and precision, and their being adorned with planets and stars."

*AS-SA`DEE: "Meaning: Seven heavens which are extremely strong, robust and firm. Allaah holds them in place with His Power, and He made them as a ceiling for the earth, and they contain many benefits for the people. So from the benefits which they contain He mentioned the sun: …"

بَنَيْنَا
We built, We raised a structure

from بَنٰى

فَوْقَ
above

سَبْعٌ
seven

شِدَادٌ
plural of شَدِيدٌ strong, firm

﴿ وَجَعَلْنَا سِرَاجًا وَهَّاجًا ﴾ (13)

*AS-SAM`AANEE: "Meaning: We have made the sun to burn and shine."

*AT-TABAREE: "He -the Most High- says: And We have made a lamp, meaning by that the sun; and His Saying: ﴿ وَهَّاجًا ﴾, meaning: burning and shining."

سِرَاجٌ
a shining lamp, a lantern.

وَهَّاجٌ
burning brightly or fiercely.

*IBN KATHEER: “Meaning: The sun, producing light which shines upon all of the people of the earth.”

*...Mujaahid[1][2] said: ﴿ وَهَّاجًا ﴾: “Shining.”

*...Qataadah[2] said: ﴿ وَهَّاجًا ﴾: “Producing light.”

*...(`Alee ibn Abee Talhah[1]: from Ibn `Abbaas: “Giving light.”)

*AL-BAGHAWEE: “…az-Zajjaaj said: *wahhaaj* means: burning.”

*AS-SA`DEE: “He draws attention, by mentioning it as being a shining lamp, to the blessing that comes about through its light, which has become something essential for the creation; and by mentioning it as ﴿ وَهَّاجًا ﴾: that which gives off heat He draws attention to the benefits of the heat it gives off.”

﴿ وَأَنزَلْنَا مِنَ ٱلْمُعْصِرَٰتِ مَآءً ثَجَّاجًا ﴾ (14)

أَنْزَلْنَا
We sent down
from أَنْزَلَ
IV root of: نَزَلَ

مُعْصِرَاتٌ
plural of مُعْصِرٌ
a cloud ready to pour forth rain

*AT-TABAREE: “﴿ ٱلْمُعْصِرَٰتِ ﴾: The most correct saying about that is to say: Allaah informed us that He sent down rain from the clouds which had become full of water, …﴿ مَآءً ثَجَّاجًا ﴾: rain which pours out continuously, just as blood pours out copiously from the body…”

[i] *...Mujaahid[1][2] said: ﴿ ٱلْمُعْصِرَٰتِ ﴾: “The wind.”

*...Qataadah[1] said: ﴿ ٱلْمُعْصِرَٰتِ ﴾: “(By means of) the winds.”

*...Ibn Zayd [1] said: ﴿ ٱلْمُعْصِرَٰتِ ﴾: "The winds."

[ii] *...(`Alee ibn Abee Talhah[1]: from Ibn `Abbaas: "The clouds.")

[iii] *...al-Hasan[1] said: "From the sky."

*...al-Qataadah[1][2] said: "From the heavens."

﴿ ثَجَّاجًا ﴾:

*...Mujaahid[1][2] said: ﴿ ثَجَّاجًا ﴾: "Poured forth."

*...Qataadah[2] said: ﴿ ثَجَّاجًا ﴾: "Poured forth."

*...(Ibn Abee Talhah[1]: from Ibn `Abbaas: "Poured forth.")

*...Ibn Zayd[1] said: "Abundant."

*IBN KATHEER: "What is most apparent is that what is meant by ﴿ ٱلْمُعْصِرَٰتِ ﴾ *al-mu`siraat* is: the clouds."

ثَجَّاجٌ flowing strongly or abundantly

from ثَجَّ

﴿ لِّنُخْرِجَ بِهِۦ حَبًّا وَنَبَاتًا ﴾ (15)

*AT-TABAREE: "He -the Most High- says: So that with the water, which We send down from the clouds to the earth, We should bring out grain…and vegetation."

"And grain (*al-Habb*) is everything that is held in the ears of cereal crops which are harvested… and as for *nabaat* (vegetation) then it is vegetation which is grazed upon, whether pasture, or plants grown from seed."

لِ in order to

نُخْرِجُ We bring out

*AL-BAGHAWEE: "﴿ حَبًّا ﴾: [[Grain]]: is what is eaten by the people, ﴿ وَنَبَاتًا ﴾ [[and vegetation]] is the plants growing from the earth, which are eaten by cattle."

from أَخْرَجَ

IV root of: خَرَجَ

*IBN KATHEER: "Meaning: So that with that plentiful, pure, beneficial, and blessed water We should bring out ﴿ حَبًّا ﴾ [[grain]] which is stored for people and cattle, ﴿ وَنَبَاتًا ﴾: meaning: green plants which are eaten fresh."

حَبٌّ corn, grain

نَبَاتٌ plants, vegetation

*AS-SA`DEE: "﴿ حَبًّا ﴾: Wheat, barley, corn, rice, and other things eaten by people. ﴿ وَنَبَاتًا ﴾: This includes all other plants which Allaah has made as food for their cattle."

﴿ وَجَنَّٰتٍ أَلْفَافًا ﴾ (16)

*AT-TABAREE: "He says: And so that with that abundant rain We should bring out gardens… and the meaning is: the fruits of gardens. So fruits were not mentioned since the Speech is sufficient to indicate that; and His Saying: ﴿ أَلْفَافًا ﴾ means: with luxuriant and dense vegetation."

*...Mujaahid[1][2] said: ﴿ أَلْفَافًا ﴾: "Entwined."

*...Qataadah[2] said: ﴿ أَلْفَافًا ﴾: "Parts of it being entwined with other parts."

جَنَّاتٌ plural of جَنَّةٌ a garden

أَلْفَافٌ luxuriant and dense vegetation

plural of لَفٌّ or لَفِيفٌ

from: لَفٌّ

*...(`Alee ibn Abee Talhah[1]: from Ibn `Abbaas: "Growing densely.")

*...Ibn Zayd[1] said: "Being entwined: some parts growing over others."

*IBN KATHEER: "Meaning: And gardens and vineyards containing fruits of various kinds and different colours, and varying fragrances, even though they grow upon a single piece of land, being gathered together ..."

*AS-SA`DEE: "Meaning: Gardens growing densely, containing all the different types of delicious fruits.

So the One Who showered these tremendous blessings upon you, blessings such that it is not possible to estimate their value, nor to count them: how can it be possible that you disbelieve in Him, and deny the Resurrection which He has informed you of?! And how can you use the blessings which He has provided you with to sin against Him, and you deny His favours?!"

*Ibnul-Jawzee in 'Zaadul-Maseer':
"The people of Tafseer said: He uses the mention of the created things as an evidence for the Resurrection. Then He informs them about the Day of Resurrection, so He -the Most High- said: ..."

﴿ إِنَّ يَوْمَ ٱلْفَصْلِ كَانَ مِيقَـٰتًا ﴾ (17)

*AT-TABAREE: "He -the Most High- says: The Day when Allaah will judge the creation, extracting justice for some from others, is an appointed time for the sentence which Allaah will apply upon those who deny the Resurrection, and upon others like them from the creation."

إِنَّ
(a word of emphasis)

يَوْمٌ day

فَصْلٌ that which separates and distinguishes

كَانَ he/it was

مِيقَاتٌ an appointed time or place

from وَقَت

*AL-BAGHAWEE: "﴿إِنَّ يَوْمَ ٱلْفَصْلِ﴾: The Day for judgement between the creation, ﴿كَانَ مِيقَـٰتًا﴾ [[is an appointed term]]: for whatever Allaah has promised regarding reward and punishment."

*IBN KATHEER: "He -the Most High- informs of the Day of Judgement, and it is the Day of Resurrection, which is set for an appointed time which will not be delayed or brought forward. No one knows its particular time except Allaah, the Mighty and Majestic ..."

*Qataadah[1] said: "It is a day which Allaah has given great honour and importance to. On that day Allaah will judge between the earlier and the later peoples, in accordance with their deeds."

*ASH-SHAWKAANEE: "Meaning: It will be a set time, a gathering, and a fixed appointment for all of the earlier and later peoples. On that Day they will come to whatever reward or punishment they were promised. It is called the Day of Decision (*al-Fasl*) since on that Day Allaah will judge between His creation. So here there begins an explanation of those matters which they disputed about with regard to the Resurrection."

*AS-SA`DEE: "He -the Most High- mentions what will occur on the Day of Resurrection, which those deniers question and which those obstinate ones reject, stating that it is a tremendous day, and that Allaah has made it a ﴿مِيقَـٰتًا﴾ [[a fixed appointment]] for the creation."

*Shaikh Muhammad ibn Saalih al-`Uthaymeen said, in his 'Tafseer Juz· `Amma':

"It is the Day of Resurrection, and it is called the Day of Decision (*al-Fasl*) since on that day Allaah will judge between the servants with regard to their disputes and that which they disagreed about. So He will distinguish between the people of the truth and the people of falsehood, the people of Unbelief and the people of Eemaan, the people of wrongdoing and transgression and the people who were justly balanced. He will also distinguish between the people of Paradise and the people of the Fire: a party will inhabit Paradise and a party will be in the Blazing Fire.

﴿ كَانَ مِيقَـٰتًا ﴾ Meaning: Appointed to occur when a certain time period has elapsed. Allaah -the Most High- says:

﴿ وَمَا نُؤَخِّرُهُۥٓ إِلَّا لِأَجَلٍ مَّعْدُودٍ ﴾

[*Soorah Hood (11): 104*]

[[Meaning: And We do not delay it except for an appointed term.]]. So what do you think about something whose delay is limited; and you yourself see how the allotted time passes quickly, day by day, until the person reaches the last stage.

Likewise this whole world, it passes day by day until it reaches the final stage. Therefore -He the Most High- said:

﴿ وَمَا نُؤَخِّرُهُۥٓ إِلَّا لِأَجَلٍ مَّعْدُودٍ ﴾

[*Soorah Hood (11): 104*]

[[Meaning: And We do not delay it except for an appointed term]]. So everything has a fixed limit and will come to an end."

﴿ يَوْمَ يُنفَخُ فِى ٱلصُّورِ فَتَأْتُونَ أَفْوَاجًا ﴾ (18)

*AT-TABAREE: "The Day of Decision will be the appointed time for what We have promised for those people:

﴿ يَوْمَ يُنفَخُ فِى ٱلصُّورِ ﴾: The Day when the Horn (*as-Soor*) will be blown ... ﴿ فَتَأْتُونَ أَفْوَاجًا ﴾ He says: So then they will come in crowds, coming in successive groups.

يُنْفَخُ
it is blown
passive form of: نَفَخَ ، يَنْفُخُ
he blew
صُورٌ
horn, hunting horn

تَأْتُون You [pl.] (will) come

from أَتَى he came

أَفْوَاجٌ

plural of فَوْجٌ a crowd, multitude

And it was said: ﴿ فَتَأْتُونَ أَفْوَاجًا ﴾ [[then you will come in crowds]] because every nation to which Allaah sent a Messenger will come along with the Messenger who was sent to them, just as He said:

﴿ يَوْمَ نَدْعُوا كُلَّ أُنَاسٍ بِإِمَـٰمِهِمْ ﴾

[*Sooratul-Israa· (17): 71*]

[[Meaning: On the Day when We call every people along with their Prophet]].”

*...Mujaahid [1][2] said: ﴿ أَفْوَاجًا ﴾: “In successive crowds.”

*AT-TIRMIDHEE reported in his ‘Sunan’ (no. 2430):
“Suwayd ibn Nasr narrated to us: `Abdullaah ibn al-Mubaarak related to us: Sulaymaan at-Taimee related to us: from Aslam al-`Ijlee: from Bishr ibn Shaghaaf: from `Abdullaah ibn `Amr ibn al-`Aas *-radiyallaahu `anhumaa-* who said: “A Bedouin came to the Prophet (ﷺ), and said: ‘What is the ‘*Soor*’?’
So he replied: << A horn which will be blown. >>”

[Saheeh: ‘Silsilatul-Ahaadeethis-Saheehah’ [no. 1080] of Shaikh Muhammad Naasiruddeen al-Albaanee].

*AL-HAAKIM reported (4/558-559), with his chain of narration: from Aboo Hurairah *-radiyallaahu `anhu-* who said: “Allaah’s Messenger (ﷺ) said: << The Angel entrusted with blowing the Horn (*as-Soor*) has been looking continuously towards the Throne, from the time he was entrusted with it, in readiness, for fear that if he glanced away he might be given the command before his glance returned to it. It is as if his eyes are two glittering stars. >>”

[Saheeh: ‘as-Saheehah’ (1078) of Shaikh al-Albaanee].

*ASH-SHAWKAANEE: “Meaning: The Day when the Horn will be blown, and it is the Horn which Israafeel will blow; and what is meant here is the second blast which is for the Resurrection.”

*AL-BUKHAAREE reported in his ‘Saheeh’ (no. 4814):
“`Umar ibn Hafs narrated to us: my father narrated to us: al-A`mash narrated to us, saying: I heard Aboo Saalih say: I heard Aboo Hurairah narrate from the Prophet (ﷺ) that he said: << Between the two blowings of the Horn there will be forty. >> The people said: ‘O Aboo Hurairah! Forty days?’ He replied: “I refuse to say (that which I have not heard).” They said: ‘Forty years?’ He said: “I refuse to say (that which I have not heard).” They said: ‘Forty months?’ He said: “I refuse to say (that which I have not heard), and he added:
<< Everything of the human body will decay except for the final bone of the coccyx, and from that bone Allaah will resurrect the human body. >>”

﴿ وَفُتِحَتِ ٱلسَّمَآءُ فَكَانَتْ أَبْوَٰبًا ﴾ **(19)**

*AT-TABAREE: “He -the Most High- says: And the heaven will be torn asunder and split open, so that it becomes path-ways, when previously it had been strong and firm, and contained no gaps or cracks; and it has been said: the meaning of that is: the heaven will be split into pieces like the pieces of timber used as doors for houses and habitations ...”

*AL-BAGHAWEE: “﴿ وَفُتِحَتِ ٱلسَّمَآءُ ﴾: The reciters of Koofah recite it without *shaddah*: ﴿ فُتِحَتْ ﴾, whereas the rest recite it with *shaddah*: ﴿ فُتِّحَتْ ﴾, meaning: it will be split open for the descent of the Angels.

﴿ فَكَانَتْ أَبْوَٰبًا ﴾: Meaning: Containing gates; and it is said: it will be undone and fall apart so that it comes to contain gates and pathways.”

فُتِحَتْ
it is (fem.) was opened
passive, from:
he opened فَتَحَ

السَّمَاءُ
the sky, heaven

كَانَتْ
she/it was

أَبْوَابٌ
plural of بَابٌ
door, gate

*AS-SAM`AANEE: "Meaning: It will be made to become pathways, or it is said: the gates of the heaven will be opened for the descent of the Angels."

*IBN KATHEER: "And the heaven will be opened so that it becomes ﴿ أَبْوَٰبًا ﴾: meaning: roads and pathways for the descent of the Angels."

ASH-SHAWKAANEE: "﴿ وَفُتِحَتِ ٱلسَّمَآءُ ﴾... It is mentioned in the past tense to indicate that it is something that is certain to occur meaning: it will be opened for the descent of the Angels.

*[[i.e. it is so certain to occur that it is as if it had already happened.]]

﴿ فَكَانَتْ أَبْوَٰبًا ﴾ is as occurs in His Saying:

﴿ وَيَوْمَ تَشَقَّقُ ٱلسَّمَآءُ بِٱلْغَمَٰمِ وَنُزِّلَ ٱلْمَلَٰٓئِكَةُ تَنزِيلًا ﴾

[*Sooratul-Furqaan (25): 25*]

[[Meaning: And the Day when heaven shall be split apart to reveal clouds, and the Angels will be sent down and descend magnificently]]... and what is meant is that it will contain many gates..."

﴿ وَسُيِّرَتِ ٱلْجِبَالُ فَكَانَتْ سَرَابًا ﴾ (20)

سُيِّرَتْ it will be made to pass away, passive form of: سَيَّرَ (he sent it/him away, he banished)

*AT-TABAREE: "He says: The mountains will be uprooted and turned to floating dust, so that they appear as a mirage: which a person from afar thinks is water, when in reality it is nothing."

*ASH-SHAWKAANEE: "Meaning: They will be made to move from their places into the air, and they will be torn up by their roots from their positions .... and He -the Perfect- has mentioned various different states for the mountains, and this is reconciled by saying:

Their first state will be their being crushed, which is His Saying:

﴿ وَحُمِلَتِ ٱلْأَرْضُ وَٱلْجِبَالُ فَدُكَّتَا دَكَّةً وَٰحِدَةً ﴾

[*Sooratul-Haaqqah (69): 14*]

[[Meaning: And the earth and the mountains will be removed from their places and crushed with a single crushing]].

Then their second state is that they become like carded wool, as in His Saying:

﴿ وَتَكُونُ ٱلْجِبَالُ كَٱلْعِهْنِ ٱلْمَنفُوشِ ﴾

[*Sooratul-Qaari`ah (101): 5*]

[[Meaning: And the mountains will be like carded wool.]]

Then the third state is that they become like floating dust, as is His Saying:

﴿ وَبُسَّتِ ٱلْجِبَالُ بَسًّا فَكَانَتْ هَبَآءً مُّنۢبَثًّا ﴾

[*Sooratul-Waaqi`ah (56): 5-6*]

[[Meaning: And the mountains will be pulverized and become floating dust]].

Then their fourth state is that they will be scattered and carried away by the winds, as occurs in His Saying:

﴿ وَتَرَى ٱلْجِبَالَ تَحْسَبُهَا جَامِدَةً وَهِىَ تَمُرُّ مَرَّ ٱلسَّحَابِ ﴾

[*Sooratun-Naml (27): 88*]

[[Meaning: And you see the mountains and think them firmly established, but they will pass away just like clouds]].

Then their fifth state is that they become a mirage: meaning they become as nothing, as occurs in this Aayah.

جِبَالٌ pl. of جَبَلٌ mountain

سَرَابٌ mirage

Then He -the Perfect- begins giving details of the decrees for that (Day of) Judgement: ...”

﴿ إِنَّ جَهَنَّمَ كَانَتْ مِرْصَادًا ﴾ (21)

جَهَنَّمُ
Hell-Fire

مِرْصَادٌ
a place of observation or ambush

*AT-TABAREE: “He -the Most High- means by His Saying that Hell-Fire lies in wait for its inhabitants: those who in this worldly life used to disbelieve in it, and for others besides them who used to believe in it; and the meaning of this Speech is that the Hell-Fire lies in wait for those who cross it, and it ambushes them.”

*...al-Hasan al-Basree[2] used to say, when he recited this Aayah: “Indeed its gate(s) have guards who are vigilant. So whoever comes with permission to proceed may pass, and whoever does not have that is imprisoned in it.”

*...Qataadah[1] said: “He informs us that there is no way into Paradise without crossing the Hell-Fire.”

*AS-SAM`AANEE: “The scholars of the language say: everything which is in front of you is a *RaSaD* [that which awaits you]; and what is meant is that it is the place where the Disbelievers will be ambushed, by the punishment that will come upon them...”

*ASH-SHAWKAANEE: “The meaning of the Aayah is that the Hell-Fire is, as decreed and ordained by Allaah, a place of ambush, where the gate-keepers of Hell will trap the Disbelievers, in order to punish them in it; or that it itself eagerly awaits those Disbelievers who are due to go to it, just as those who have set up an ambush lie in wait for those who pass by.”

﴿ لِّلطَّٰغِينَ مَـَٔابًا ﴾ (22)

*AT-TABAREE: "He -the Most High- says: Hell-Fire will be for those who were impious transgressors in the world, those who transgressed the limits set by Allaah, those who behaved insolently towards their Lord. It will be for them an abode to which they must return, and a place which they must go to and inhabit."

*...Qataadah[1]: "Meaning: An abode and place of residence."

*AL-BAGHAWEE: "﴿ لِّلطَّٰغِينَ ﴾: For the Disbelievers, ﴿ مَـَٔابًا ﴾: a place to which they must return."

*IBN KATHEER: "﴿ لِّلطَّٰغِينَ ﴾: They are the obstinate and rebellious sinners who contradicted the Messengers, ﴿ مَـَٔابًا ﴾: meaning: a place of return, a final destination, a final residence and an alighting place."

*ASH-SHAWKAANEE: "*at-Taaghee* is the one who transgresses with Disbelief (Kufr)."

*Shaikh Ibn `Uthaymeen said in his 'Tafseer Juz· `Amma':
"*at-Tughyaan* (transgression) means to exceed the limit, and the limit and goal laid down for man is mentioned in the Saying of Allaah -the Most High:

﴿ وَمَا خَلَقْتُ ٱلْجِنَّ وَٱلْإِنسَ إِلَّا لِيَعْبُدُونِ ﴾

[*Sooratudh-Dhaariyaat (51): 56*]

[[Meaning: And I have not created jinn and mankind except that they should worship Me alone]]. So whoever exceeds his limit and does not worship Allaah alone, then he is an impious transgressor, so Hell-Fire will be their destination and final resting place."

طَاغُون

plural of طَاغِي

a transgressor, one who goes beyond all limits in sin, one who is excessively impious

from طَغَى

he/it exceeded the bounds

مَئَابٌ

a place of return

from آب

﴿ لَّٰبِثِينَ فِيهَآ أَحْقَابًا ﴾ (23)

لَابِثٌ one who remains at a place

from لَبِث

فِيهَا in it

أَحْقَابٌ plural of حُقُبٌ a very long period of time, an aeon, ages

*AT-TABAREE: "He -the Most High- says: Those who were impious transgressors in the worldly life will remain in Hell-Fire, staying therein for aeons."

*...Aboo Hurairah[1]-*radiyallaahu `anhu*- said: "A *huqub* will be eighty years, and a year will be three hundred and sixty days, and each day will be a thousand years."

*...Qataadah[2]: "It reached us that a *huqub* is eighty years long, from the years of the Hereafter."

*...Qataadah[1]: "There will be no end to that: whenever one aeon is completed another one comes after it, and it was mentioned to us that a *huqub* is eighty years."

*AL-BAGHAWEE: "A single *huqub* will be eighty years: each year being of twelve months, each month being of thirty days, and each day being a thousand years..."

AT-TABAREE: "So if it is said that the Disbelievers will only be punished by Allaah for aeons [and no longer], then the response is that ar-Rabee` [ibn Anas al-Bakree, *taabi`ee: d. 139H] and Qataadah both said that these aeons will never cease and never finish. So it is possible that the meaning of this is: they will remain for aeons suffering this type of torment, which is:

﴿ لَّا يَذُوقُونَ فِيهَا بَرْدًا وَلَا شَرَابًا إِلَّا حَمِيمًا وَغَسَّاقًا ﴾

[*Aayahs 24-25*]

[[Meaning: They will not taste therein anything to reduce the heat of the blazing Fire for them, except the pus of the wounds of those suffering in the Fire; nor any drink to quench their severe thirst, except for boiling fluid]], so when these aeons are completed they will then go on to suffer other types of punishment, just as Allaah -the Majestic- said in His Book:

﴿ وَإِنَّ لِلطَّٰغِينَ لَشَرَّ مَـَٔابٍ جَهَنَّمَ يَصْلَوْنَهَا فَبِئْسَ ٱلْمِهَادُ هَٰذَا فَلْيَذُوقُوهُ حَمِيمٌ وَغَسَّاقٌ وَءَاخَرُ مِن شَكْلِهِۦٓ أَزْوَٰجٌ ﴾

[*Soorah Saad (38): 55-58*]

[[Meaning: And for the rebellious and impious transgressors there will be an evil final destination: Hell-Fire, where they will burn, and what an evil resting place. This is boiling fluid and the pus of wounds, so let them taste it! And other torments like it, of different kinds]], so this saying is, in my view, closest with respect to the meaning of the Aayah."

*ASH-SHAWKAANEE: "Meaning: They will remain in the Fire for as long as the aeons continue, and the aeons will never cease: whenever one is completed another begins."

﴿ لَّا يَذُوقُونَ فِيهَا بَرْدًا وَلَا شَرَابًا ﴾ (24)

﴿ إِلَّا حَمِيمًا وَغَسَّاقًا ﴾ (25)

*AT-TABAREE: "They will not taste in it anything cool to reduce the heat of the blazing Fire for them, except for *ghassaaq* [the pus flowing from the wounds of the inhabitants of Hell], nor any drink to quench the severe thirst they suffer except for *hameem* [boiling hot fluid].

Then some of those having knowledge of the speech of the Arabs say that *al-bard* (coolness) here means sleep....so sleep is therefore sometimes called *bard* (coolness). But this is not its well-known name; and the Book of Allaah should be explained in accordance with the predominant usage from what is well-known from the speech of the Arabs, to the exclusion of other than it."

يَذُوقُونَ
they (will) taste, (taste punishment)
from ذَاقَ

بَرْدٌ
cold, coolness

شَرَابٌ
a drink

حَمِيمٌ
boiling water, scalding hot fluid

غَسَّاقٌ
dark and murky fluid, the pus flowing from the wounds of the inhabitants of the Fire

from غَسَقَ
it trickled and was dark

*...Ibraaheem an-Nakha`ee[1] and Aboo Razeen[1] said:

"﴿ وَغَسَّاقًا ﴾ Is the pus that flows from (the wounds of) the people of the Fire."

*...Qataadah[1] said: "It used to be said to us that *al-ghassaaq* is that which flows from between the skin and the flesh."

*...Sufyaan ath-Thawree[2] said: "﴿ وَغَسَّاقًا ﴾: It reached me that it is the tears that flow from them."

*...Ibn Zayd[1] said: "*al-Hameem* is the tears flowing from their eyes into the Fire which gather in trenches. They are then given this to drink' and *al-ghassaaq* is the pus which flows from their wounds, caused by the scorching of the Fire. This is gathered in troughs and given to them to drink."

*...[`Alee ibn Abee Talhah[1]: from ibn `Abbaas: ﴿ وَغَسَّاقًا ﴾, he said: "It is *az-Zamhareer* (a bitterly cold fluid)."]

*AT-TABAREE: "﴿ وَغَسَّاقًا ﴾: And what we must say is: that which Allaah has promised those people, and the drink that He has mentioned they will taste in the Hereafter is that bitterly cold fluid in Hell-Fire (*az-Zamhareer*), which combines intense cold and putrid stench..."

*AL-BAGHAWEE: "*al-ghassaaq* is the bitterly cold fluid that will burn them with its coldness, and it is said: it is the pus flowing from the inhabitants of the Fire."

*AS-SAM`AANEE: "﴿ إِلَّا حَمِيمًا وَغَسَّاقًا ﴾: Aboo `Ubaydah said: "*al-Hameem* is hot water"... and it is said: *al-Hameem* is their tears which are gathered and given to them to drink; and His Saying: ﴿ وَغَسَّاقًا ﴾ meaning: thick pus, and it is said that it is the pus flowing from the wounds of the inhabitants of the Fire.

It is also said: *al-Hameem* is a fluid at the peak of intense heat; whereas *al-Ghassaaq* is at the limit of extreme coldness, and it is *az-Zamhareer*: so they are punished with both these torments."

*IBN KATHEER: "Meaning: They will not find in Hell-Fire anything cool for their hearts, nor any wholesome drink by which they can be nourished. Therefore, He -the Most High- said:

﴿ إِلَّا حَمِيمًا وَغَسَّاقًا ﴾: Abul-`Aaliyah [[Rufai` ibn Mihraan: taabi`ee, d. 93 H]] said: "So He excepted from the coolness *al-Hameem*, and from the drinks *al-Ghassaaq*; and ar-Rabee` ibn Anas said likewise. So as for 'al-*H*ameem' then it is that liquid which is so hot that it has reached the ultimate limit of intense heat; and *al-Ghassaaq* is whatever has gathered from the blood and pus flowing from the inhabitants of the Fire, and their sweat, tears, and the putrid discharge of their wounds: and it is so severely cold that it cannot be drunk, and its putrid stench is so awful that it cannot be faced."

*AS-SA`DEE: "﴿ لَّا يَذُوقُونَ فِيهَا بَرْدًا وَلَا شَرَابًا ﴾: meaning: they will have nothing to cool their skins, and nothing to quench their thirst, ﴿ إِلَّا حَمِيمًا ﴾ meaning: (except) hot water which will scald their faces and consume their intestines, (and) ﴿ وَغَسَّاقًا ﴾: which is the pus flowing from the inhabitants of the Fire, and is extremely repulsive in its odour, and extremely foul in its taste. "

Aboo Moosaa al-Ash`aree *-radiyallaahu `anhu- reported that Allaah's Messenger (ﷺ) said: << The inhabitants of the Fire will weep to such an extent that ships could sail in their tears, and they will weep blood-meaning: in place of tears. >>

[Hasan lighairihi: Reported by al-Haakim (4/605): 'as-Saheehah': 1679]

جَزَآءً وِفَاقًا (26)

جَزَآء

recompense, retribution, reward

وِفَاقٌ

fitting

*AL-BAGHAWEE: "Meaning: We will give them retribution which befits their deeds."

*AT-TABAREE: "He -the Most High- says: This punishment, which will be given to those Disbelievers in the Hereafter, will be given to them by their Lord as recompense; meaning: as retribution for them for their wicked deeds and sayings in the worldly life."

*...Mujaahid[1][2] said: "The recompense exactly fits the deeds."

*...(`Alee ibn Abee Talhah[1] from Ibn `Abbaas: "Befitting their deeds.")

*...Qataadah[1] said: "The recompense fully befits the evil actions which those people committed."

*...Ibn Zayd[1] said: "They committed evil and so were recompensed with evil, and (others) did good deeds and so were rewarded with good ..."

* Shirk: Directing any act of worship to other than Allaah.

*AL-BAGHAWEE: "Meaning: We will give them a recompense which befits their deeds. Muqaatil said: "The punishment befits the sin; so there is no sin greater than *Shirk, and there is no punishment greater than the Fire."

*AS-SA`DEE: "They fully deserved these terrible punishments as a fitting recompense for the deeds they committed which led them to it. Allaah did not wrong them; rather they wronged their own souls. He therefore mentions their actions, for which they fully deserved this punishment: ..."

﴿ إِنَّهُمْ كَانُوا۟ لَا يَرْجُونَ حِسَابًا ﴾ **(27)**

*AT-TABAREE: "He -the Most High- says: Those Disbelievers, whilst they were in the world, had not used to fear that Allaah would call them to account for the favours that He granted them, and His fine treatment of them, and for their ingratitude towards Him for that."

*...Mujaahid[1][2] said: "They did not care, and therefore they did not believe in the affairs of the Hidden and Unseen (*al-Ghayb*)."

*...Qataadah[1] said: "They did not fear any reckoning."

*...Ibn Zayd[1] said: "They did not believe in the Resurrection, nor in the Reckoning; and how can one who does not believe that he will be restored to life and resurrected, hope or fear the Reckoning?!.."

*AL-BAGHAWEE: "They did not fear that they would be brought to account; and the meaning is that they had not used to believe in the Resurrection, nor that they would face a reckoning."

*AS-SAM`AANEE: "Meaning: They did not fear it; and we have already explained *rajaa·* can mean fear."

*AS-SA`DEE: "They did not believe in the Resurrection, nor that Allaah would repay the creation with good and evil. So therefore they left aside performing deeds for the Hereafter."

يَرْجُونَ
they hope, expect or fear

from رَجٰو

حِسَابٌ
a reckoning, an account

﴿ وَكَذَّبُوا۟ بِـَٔايَـٰتِنَا كِذَّابًا ﴾ (28)

كَذَّبُوا

They denied, belied, called something a lie, or they called someone a liar.

from كَذَّبَ

II root of: كَذَبَ

آياتٌ

plural of آيَةٌ

a proof, a sign

*AT-TABAREE: "He -the Most High- says: And those Disbelievers denied Our proofs and Our signs."

*IBN KATHEER: "Meaning: They used to deny Allaah's signs and His proofs upon His creation, which He sent down to His Messenger (ﷺ). So they met these with denial and obstinate rejection."

*AS-SA`DEE: "Meaning: They denied them with a clear and open denial; and the clear proofs came to them, but they obstinately rejected them."

*Shaikh `Uthaymeen said in his 'Tafseer Juz· `Amma':

"They denied. They said: 'this is lies', 'this is sorcery,' 'this is lunacy,' and the like of that, as is mentioned in the Book of Allaah with regard to the descriptions which those rejecters applied to the Messengers of Allaah…; and their people who called them liars did not limit themselves to that; rather they caused physical harm to them, just as they did with the Messenger (ﷺ) to whom they caused great harm. Indeed they even took up arms against them, so the recompense for such people is Hell-Fire: a fitting recompense for their deeds."

(29) ﴿ وَكُلَّ شَىْءٍ أَحْصَيْنَـٰهُ كِتَـٰبًا ﴾

*AL-BAGHAWEE: "Meaning: And We clearly recorded all actions in the Preserved Tablet (al-Lawhul-Mahfooz), just like His Saying:

﴿ وَكُلَّ شَىْءٍ أَحْصَيْنَـٰهُ فِىٓ إِمَامٍ مُّبِينٍ ﴾

[*Soorah YaaSeen (36): 12*]

[[Meaning: We have carefully recorded everything in the Preserved Tablet]]."

*AT-TABAREE: "He -the Most High- says: And We have encompassed everything and written it in a Book; writing down its number, limit and measure. So nothing escapes Us from knowledge of that."

*IBN KATHEER: "Meaning: We have known all the actions of the servants and have written them down for them, and We will recompense them for that: if good, then with good; and if evil, then with evil."

*Shaikh `Atiyyah Muhammad Saalim said in his completion of 'Adwaa· ul-Bayaan' of Shaikh Muhammad al-Ameen ash-Shanqeetee:

"It is said that what is meant by ﴿ شَىْءٍ ﴾ [[thing(s)]] here is: the deeds of the people. So that after His Saying ﴿ جَزَآءً وِفَاقًا ﴾: meaning: [[a retribution]] fully befitting their deeds, without any increase or decrease, He said: And We have precisely recorded and written down their deeds."

*AS-SA`DEE: "﴿ وَكُلَّ شَىْءٍ ﴾ [[and everything]]: whether it be a small amount or a large amount, good or evil: ﴿ أَحْصَيْنَـٰهُ كِتَـٰبًا ﴾:

كُلٌّ
every, all…

شَيْءٌ
a thing

أَحْصَيْنَا
We enumerated, took account of, recorded, retained, encompassed

from أَحْصَى

IV root of: حَصَا

كِتَابٌ
a book, a written record

meaning: We have recorded it in a Preserved Tablet. So the wrongdoers need not fear that We will punish them for sins which they did not commit. Nor should they imagine that any of their [evil] deeds will be missed, or that even an atom's weight will be forgotten from them. Just as Allaah -the Most High- said:

﴿ وَوُضِعَ ٱلْكِتَٰبُ فَتَرَى ٱلْمُجْرِمِينَ مُشْفِقِينَ مِمَّا فِيهِ وَيَقُولُونَ يَٰوَيْلَتَنَا مَالِ هَٰذَا ٱلْكِتَٰبِ لَا يُغَادِرُ صَغِيرَةً وَلَا كَبِيرَةً إِلَّآ أَحْصَىٰهَا ۚ وَوَجَدُوا۟ مَا عَمِلُوا۟ حَاضِرًا ۗ وَلَا يَظْلِمُ رَبُّكَ أَحَدًا ﴾

[*Sooratul-Kahf (18): 49*]

[[Meaning: The record of the servants deeds will be placed in their hands and you will see the sinful Mushrikoon fearful of what is recorded therein. Then when they have read the sins written against them they will say: 'Woe to us! What sort of a book is this which leaves no sin, small or large, except that it records it; and they will find all their deeds recorded in that book; and your Lord will not treat anyone unjustly.]]."

﴿ فَذُوقُوا۟ فَلَن نَّزِيدَكُمْ إِلَّا عَذَابًا ﴾ (30)

ذُوقُوا
taste! (plural)

from ذَاقَ
he tasted (punishment)

لَنْ
(a denial of something occurring in the future)

*AT-TABAREE: "He -the Majestic- says: It will be said to those Disbelievers in the Hell-Fire, when they drink the boiling fluid and foul pus: Taste, O people, the punishment of Allaah which you used to deny in the worldly life; because We will not give you anything except increase in punishment, on top of the punishment which you are already suffering. It will not be reduced for you, nor will it be made any easier for you to bear.

*...`Abdullaah ibn `Amr[1]- *radiyallaahu `anhumaa-* said: "No Aayah has been sent down which is more severe upon the inhabitants of the Fire than this Aayah:

﴿ فَذُوقُواْ فَلَن نَّزِيدَكُمْ إِلَّا عَذَابًا ﴾. So they will continually have their punishment increased, forever."

*IBN KATHEER: "It will be said to the inhabitants of the Fire: taste what you are suffering, because We will not give you anything except an increase of the same type of punishment, and other types of punishment as well."

*ASH-SHAWKAANEE: "This sentence is stated as a result of their Disbelief and their rejection of the signs. ar-Raazee said: This (*faa·*) ﴿ فَ ﴾ [[so, therefore…]]: expresses recompense. So He indicated that the command for them to taste had as its reason their foul deeds, which have already been explained. Then from the increase in their punishment is that whenever their skins are burnt away they will have them replaced with new skins, and whenever the Fire begins to abate, then Allaah will make it blaze even more fiercely."*

*AS-SA`DEE: "﴿ فَذُوقُواْ ﴾ [[then taste]]: O you deniers, this painful punishment and this perpetual disgrace and humiliation…"

*Shaikh Ibn `Uthaymeen said in his 'Tafseer Juz· `Amma':
"This command is given to humiliate and rebuke them, meaning: it will be said to the inhabitants of the Fire: Taste the punishment as a humiliation and a rebuke, for We will only increase you in punishment, and We will never reduce it for you. Indeed We will not even leave you upon your present level of punishment; rather We will increase it in severity, its length and its type. Then it is mentioned in another Aayah that they will say to the gate-keepers of Hell-Fire:

﴿ ٱدْعُواْ رَبَّكُمْ يُخَفِّفْ عَنَّا يَوْمًا مِّنَ ٱلْعَذَابِ ﴾

[*Soorah Ghaafir (40): 49*]

[[Meaning: Call upon your Lord to lighten our torment for a single day]]. So consider this Saying from a number of aspects:

نَزِيدُ
we increase
from زَادَ

إِلاَّ
except

عَذَابٌ
punishment, torment

*See Sooratun-Nisaa· (4): 56; and Sooratul-Israa· (17): 97

Firstly: They will not ask Allaah -the Perfect and Most High- rather they will ask the gate-keepers of Hell-Fire to supplicate for them, because Allaah has said to them:

﴿ قَالَ ٱخۡسَـُٔواْ فِيهَا وَلَا تُكَلِّمُونِ ﴾

[*Sooratul-Mu·minoon (23): 108*]

[[Meaning: Remain therein in disgrace, and do not speak to Me]]. So they see themselves as being unfitting to ask Allaah, and to supplicate to Him, except via an intermediary.

Secondly: They will say: ﴿ ٱدۡعُواْ رَبَّكُمۡ ﴾ [[call upon **your** Lord]], and they will not say: 'call upon **our** Lord', because their faces and hearts will be unable to mention ascription of Allaah's Lordship with respect to themselves, such that they would say 'our Lord.' So it will be from their state of humiliation and disgrace that they will see themselves as unbefitting of having Allaah's Lordship mentioned in relation to themselves. Rather they will say: 'your Lord'.

Thirdly: They will not say: 'to **remove** our torment', rather they will say: ﴿ يُخَفِّفۡ ﴾ [[to lighten it]], since they are in despair, and Allaah's refuge is sought. They have totally despaired of its being removed from them.

Fourthly: They will not say: 'to lighten our torment **forever**', rather they will say: ﴿ يَوۡمًا مِّنَ ٱلۡعَذَابِ ﴾ [[to lighten our torment for a single day]]: a single day! So this makes clear the level of torment, humiliation, and disgrace they will suffer.

﴿ وَتَرَىٰهُمۡ يُعۡرَضُونَ عَلَيۡهَا خَٰشِعِينَ مِنَ ٱلذُّلِّ يَنظُرُونَ مِن طَرۡفٍ خَفِيٍّ ﴾

[*Sooratush-Shooraa(42): 45*]

[[Meaning: And you will see the wrongdoers being exposed to the Hell-Fire: humbled and fearful, in a state of humiliation, stealing glances towards the Fire]].

May Allaah save us from that."

﴿ إِنَّ لِلْمُتَّقِينَ مَفَازًا ﴾ (31)

*AT-TABAREE: "Those who fear and revere Allaah, and are obedient to Him (*al-Muttaqoon*) will attain a place of safety and security from the Hell-Fire, being granted Paradise, and they will be successful in attaining what they sought."

*...Mujaahid[1][2] said: "They succeeded in being saved from the Fire."

*...Qataadah[1] said: "Yes, by Allaah, being saved from the Fire and attaining Paradise; and being saved from Allaah's punishment, and attaining His Mercy."

*...(`Alee ibn Abee Talhah[1]: from Ibn `Abbaas: ﴿ مَفَازًا ﴾, he said: "A place of enjoyment.")

*IBN KATHEER: "Allaah -the Most High- says, informing about the people of bliss, and about the honour and perpetual bliss which He -the Most High- has prepared for them. So He -the Most High- says: ﴿ إِنَّ لِلْمُتَّقِينَ مَفَازًا ﴾. Ibn `Abbaas and ad-Dahhaak said that it means: a place of enjoyment, whereas Mujaahid and Qataadah said: they succeeded in that they were saved from the Fire. However what is most apparent here is the saying of Ibn `Abbaas, because after it He said: ﴿ حَدَآئِقَ ﴾ [[walled gardens…]]."

*ASH-SHAWKAANEE: "Here there begins an explanation of the condition of the Believers, and of the good which Allaah has prepared for them; after the condition of the Disbelievers and the evil which Allaah has made ready for them has been explained. So

الْمُتَّقُونَ
those who possess 'taqwaa': those who fear, revere and are dutiful to Allaah: doing whatever He has commanded, and avoiding whatever He has forbidden.

from اِتَّقَى

VIII root of: وَقَى

he protected himself, he was on his guard.

مَفَازٌ، فَوْزٌ
success and salvation

from فَازَ
he succeeded

al-mafaaz is a verbal noun meaning: successful attainment of Favour, and of that which was sought, and salvation from the Fire."

*AS-SA`DEE: "Having mentioned the state of the transgressors He then mentioned the destination of those who fear, revere and are dutiful to Allaah, so He said: ﴿إِنَّ لِلْمُتَّقِينَ مَفَازًا﴾ meaning: those who fear and beware of the Anger of their Lord, by adhering to obedience to Him, and by withholding from whatever He detests, then they will attain success and salvation, and they will be removed far away from the Fire; and in this lies their success and salvation."

*Shaikh Ibn `Uthaymeen said in his 'Tafseer Juz· `Amma':

"Allaah -the Mighty and Majestic- mentioned the bliss which the *Muttaqoon* will enjoy after His Saying:

﴿إِنَّ جَهَنَّمَ كَانَتْ مِرْصَادًا لِّلطَّـٰغِينَ مَـَٔابًا﴾

[*Aayahs 21-22*]

[[Meaning: Hell-Fire lies in wait for its inhabitants: for the impious transgressors it will be an abode which they must inhabit]],
since the Qur·aan mentions things in pairs: when He mentions punishment in it He mentions reward also; and when He mentions reward He also mentions punishment. Likewise when He mentions the doers of good, He also mentions the evildoers; and when He mentions the truth, He mentions falsehood. So opposites are mentioned along with each other so that the person will proceed towards his Lord between fear and hope. Since if hope overcomes a person he will feel safe against Allaah's plan, and if he is overcome by fear then he will fall into despairing of Allaah's Mercy; and both of these are major sins, and both of them are evils. Imaam Ahmad ibn Hanbal - *rahimahullaah*- said: "A person should, in worshipping his Lord, be between fear and hope, and if one of them overcomes then it will destroy the person." Therefore you will find the Noble Qur·aan mentioning this along with that. Also for the reason that peoples' souls should not become weary of continual mention of a single condition and its detailed elaboration, without any mention of its opposite. Likewise so that when a person recites the Qur·aan he

will be in a state of desire and of fear. So this is from the eloquence of the Noble Qur·aan."

﴿ حَدَآئِقَ وَأَعۡنَٰبٗا ﴾ (32)

*AT-TABAREE: "﴿ حَدَآئِقَ ﴾:'The walled gardens': this is an explanation and clarification of the success (*mafaaz*). So it is permissible [linguistically] for this to occur as an explanation for it, since the *mafaaz* is a verbal noun used in a person's saying: 'So and so succeeded (*faaza*) in something', when he sought and was successful in attaining it. So it is as if it is being said: Those who fear and revere Allaah, and are obedient to Him will be successful in attaining what they sought: walled gardens and grape-vines. And *hadaa·iq* is the plural of *hadeeqah*, and it is gardens of date-palms, grape-vines and trees, surrounded by enclosing walls. So it is called a *hadeeqah* (walled garden) because of its being enclosed and surrounded (*ihdaaq*) by walls. So if it is not surrounded by walls, then it is not called a *hadeeqah*...; and His Saying: ﴿ وَأَعۡنَٰبٗا ﴾ means: grape-vines, and the mention of grapes (*a`naab*) renders it unnecessary to mention the vines."

حَدائِقُ plural of حَدِيقَةٌ a walled garden

أَعْنَابٌ plural of عِنَبٌ grapes

*AL-BAGHAWEE: "Meaning: The trees and fruits of Paradise."

*AS-SA`DEE: "﴿ حَدَآئِقَ ﴾: And they are gardens which gather all types of beautiful trees with fruits, and between them flow rivers ﴿ وَأَعۡنَٰبٗا ﴾: and grapes are specifically mentioned because of their distinction, and because of their abundance in those gardens."

Shaikh Ibn `Uthaymeen said: "﴿ حَدَآئِقَ وَأَعۡنَٰبٗا ﴾: This describes the type of the success; ﴿ حَدَآئِقَ ﴾: meaning: gardens containing huge and plentiful trees of different kinds, ﴿وَأَعۡنَٰبٗا﴾: *al-a`naab is the plural of *`inab* (grapes) and they are included within the plants growing in the walled gardens, however they are mentioned in particular."

﴿وَكَوَاعِبَ أَتۡرَابٗا﴾ (33)

كَوَاعِبُ
plural of كَاعِبٌ
a woman with full, raised and prominent breasts

أَتْرَابٌ
plural of تِرْبٌ
a companion of equal age

*AT-TABAREE: "And full-breasted maidens of equal age."

*...Qataadah[1][2] said: "Full-breasted women of equal age."

*...[`Alee ibn Abee Talhah[1]: from Ibn `Abbaas: ﴿وَكَوَاعِبَ﴾ he said: "And full-breasted maidens; and His Saying: ﴿أَتۡرَابٗا﴾: of equal age."]

*...Ibn Zayd[1] said: "*al-Kawaakib* means the woman whose breasts are raised and full/prominent" and he said: ﴿أَتۡرَابٗا﴾: means: of equal age."

*IBN KATHEER: "Meaning: Full-breasted maidens, which mean that their breasts are raised and full; not drooping, since they are amorous virgins of equal age."

*AS-SAM`AANEE: "﴿أَتۡرَابٗا﴾: Meaning: Maidens equal in age; and it is said that they will be thirty three years old."

*Aboo Nu`aym reported in 'Sifatul-Jannah' (2/106), and al-Bukhaaree in 'at-Taareekhul-Kabeer' (4/2/219/no. 2779), by way of `Umar ibn `Abdul-Waahid: from al-Awzaa`ee: from Haaroon ibn

Ri·aab: from Anas ibn Maalik -*radiyallaahu ‘anhu*- who said: Allaah’s Messenger (ﷺ) said:
<< The people will be raised on the Day of Resurrection in the form of Aadam: hairless, beardless, with eyelids edged with black; being thirty-three years old. Then they will be brought to a tree in Paradise and be clothed from it. Their clothes will not wear out and their youth will not pass away. >>

[Shaikh al-Albaanee said in as-Saheehah’ (6/1/46): “Its chain of narration is ‘Saheeh’.”]

*AS-SA`DEE: “And they will have wives therein, in accordance with their souls’ desires: ﴿ وَكَوَاعِبَ ﴾: and they are maidens with full breasts. So because of their youthfulness, vitality, and freshness, their breasts have not sagged; and ﴿ أَتْرَابًا ﴾ means: women of equal age, close to each other; and it is usual that those of equal age will be in harmony and able to live together, and this age is thirty three years which is the most justly balanced age of youth.”

﴿ وَكَأْسًا دِهَاقًا ﴾ (34)

*AT-TABAREE: “And a cup filled to the brim, brought one after the other for the drinkers; being numerous and full.”

*...Aboo Hurairah -*radiyallaahu ‘anhu*[2] said: “Brought one after the other.”

*...Mujaahid[1][2] said: “Brought one after the other.”

*...Mujaahid[3][9] said: “﴿ دِهَاقًا ﴾: Full.”
*...al-Hasan al-Basree[1] said: “Full.”

*...Qataadah[1][2][3] said: “Full to the brim.”

كَأْسٌ
a cup (containing drink)

دِهَاقٌ
full to the brim

*...Ibn Zayd[1] said: "Full."

*AL-BUKHAAREE reported [Book of the Virtues of the Ansaar]: (no. 3839): "Ishaaq ibn Ibraaheem narrated to me, saying: I said to Aboo Usaamah: Yahyaa ibn al-Muhallib narrated to you: Husayn narrated to us: from `Ikrimah: ﴿وَكَأْسًا دِهَاقًا﴾, he said: "Full, and coming in succession."

*AS-SA`DEE: "Meaning: Full of heavenly wine (*raheeq*), delicious for those who drink it."

◈

﴿لَّا يَسْمَعُونَ فِيهَا لَغْوًا وَلَا كِذَّٰبًا﴾ (35)

يَسْمَعُونَ
they (will) hear

لَغْوٌ
useless and vain speech...

كِذَّابًا
lying, accusation of falsehood

*AT-TABAREE: "He-the Most High-says: In Paradise they shall not hear false and futile speech, nor accusations of falsehood; meaning: they will not accuse each other of telling lies."

*AS-SAM`AANEE: "*al-Laghw* is futile speech, and His Saying: ﴿كِذَّٰبًا﴾: means: they will not accuse each other of telling lies; and it was also recited ﴿كِذَابًا﴾..., and its meaning is falsehood ...."

*IBN KATHEER: "It is like His Saying:

﴿لَّا لَغْوٌ فِيهَا وَلَا تَأْثِيمٌ﴾
[*Sooratut-Toor (52): 23*]

[[Meaning: They will not speak therein with any useless speech, nor with sinful speech]], meaning: there will be no speech therein that is futile, containing no benefit; nor the sin of telling lies. Rather it is the abode of peace and security, and everything within it is free of deficiency."

*Ibnul-Jawzee said in ‘Zaadul-Maseer’: “﴿ لَّا يَسْمَعُونَ فِيهَا ﴾ [[Meaning: They will not hear therein…]] meaning: in Paradise, when they drink: ﴿ لَغْوًا ﴾ [[futile speech]]...﴿ وَلَا كِذَّابًا ﴾: meaning: they will not call each other liars. So when the people drink wine in the world they speak with futile speech, whereas the inhabitants of Paradise are free of that.”

﴿ جَزَآءً مِّن رَّبِّكَ عَطَآءً حِسَابًا ﴾ (36)

*AT-TABAREE: “Allaah will give those who fear, revere and obey Him what has been described in these Aayahs, as a reward from your Lord for their deeds: for their obedience to Him in the worldly life; and His Saying ﴿ عَطَآءً ﴾ means that Allaah gives them this reward as a generous gift. This is because He rewards a single good deed from them with ten rewards in some cases, and with seven hundred rewards in other cases. So this increase, even though it is a reward, is a generous gift, and His Saying ﴿ حِسَابًا ﴾ means: as a recompense for them for the deeds which they did for Allaah in the world.”

*...Mujaahid[1][2] said: “As a bestowal from Him in recompense for the deeds they did.”

*...Qataadah[1] said: “Meaning: As an abundant bestowal. So He will reward them for slight actions with a tremendous amount of good that will never cease.”

*IBN KATHEER: “Meaning: What We have mentioned will be given to them by Allaah as a reward, and He will grant it to them by

جَزَاءٌ
reward, recompense

رَبُّكَ
your Lord (Who nurtures & sustains)

رَبٌّ
Lord

عَطَاءٌ
a gift, grant, a favour

حِسَاباً
recompense

His Bounty, His Favour, His Beneficence and His Mercy; as a gift that is ﴿ حِسَابًا ﴾."

*ASH-SHAWKAANEE: "*al-hisaab* means 'as has been decreed'; meaning: in accordance with the amount decreed for him in the promise of the Lord -the One free of all imperfections. So He promised to reward a good deed with ten times its like, and He promised that some people will be rewarded with seven hundred times its like: with a reward that will never end and is unlimited, as in His Saying:

﴿ إِنَّمَا يُوَفَّى ٱلصَّٰبِرُونَ أَجْرَهُم بِغَيْرِ حِسَابٍ ﴾

[*Sooratuz-Zumar (39): 10*]

[[Meaning: Allaah will reward those who were patient with a reward that is without measure]]."

*Shaikh `Atiyyah Muhammad Saalim said in his completion of Shaikh Muhammad al-Ameen ash-Shanqeetee's 'Adwaa· ul-Bayaan':

"He said with regard to the Disbelievers: ﴿ جَزَآءً وِفَاقًا ﴾ [*Aayah 26*] [[Meaning: A retribution befitting their deeds]],

but regarding the Believers He said: ﴿ عَطَآءً حِسَابًا ﴾ [[Meaning: As a generous gift]].

So the first case makes clear that their retribution is in full accordance with their deeds, and your Lord does not wrong or oppress anyone.

Whereas in the second case there is an explanation that this bliss is a gift from Allaah, and is a great favour upon them from Him, in addition to the basic favour which is the salvation (*al-mafaaz*) explained in the Saying of Allaah -the Most High:

﴿ فَمَن زُحْزِحَ عَنِ ٱلنَّارِ وَأُدْخِلَ ٱلْجَنَّةَ فَقَدْ فَازَ ﴾

[*Soorah Aal-`Imraan (3): 185*]

[[Meaning: And whoever is kept away from the Fire and entered into Paradise then he has truly succeeded]].

So entry into Paradise is in itself a gift from Allaah, as occurs in the hadeeth: << None of you will enter Paradise by his deeds. >>

[[Reported by al-Bukhaaree (no. 6464) and Muslim, as a hadeeth of `Aa·ishah -*radiyallaahu `anhaa.*]]

Then His Saying: ﴿ حِسَابًا ﴾ [[as recompense]] contains an indication that the different levels of the people of Paradise within Paradise are in accordance with their due recompense, and are a result of their deeds. It is also said: *hisaaban* means: fully sufficient, as if each one of them says: 'It is fully sufficient for me'."

﴿ رَّبِّ ٱلسَّمَٰوَٰتِ وَٱلْأَرْضِ وَمَا بَيْنَهُمَا ٱلرَّحْمَٰنِ لَا يَمْلِكُونَ

مِنْهُ خِطَابًا ﴾ (37)

*AT-TABAREE: "He -the Majestic- says: As a reward from your Lord and Nurturer: the Lord of the seven heavens and of the earth, and of whatever of the creation is between them: the Extremely Merciful One… None from His creation will be able to address Him on the Day of Resurrection except for those He permits from them, and who speak with what is correct."

*...Mujaahid[1][2] said: "﴿ خِطَابًا ﴾: With speech."

*...Qataadah[1] said: "Meaning: With speech."

*...Ibn Zayd [1] said: "They will be unable to initiate any address with Allaah, meaning: to plea or argue on behalf of someone."

سَمَاوَاتٌ
plural of سَمَاءٌ heaven

الأَرْضُ
the earth

بَيْنَ
between

هُمَا
the two of them

الرَّحْمٰنُ
the Extremely Merciful (Allaah)

يَمْلِكُون

they (will) possess, own, are able to do…

from مَلَك

خِطَابٌ

an address, speech

*IBN KATHEER: "He -the Most High- informs of His Magnificence and Majesty, and that He is the Lord of the heavens and the earth and of whatever they contain, and whatever lies between them; and that He is the Extremely Merciful One, Who is such that His Mercy encompasses everything; and His Saying:

﴿ لَا يَمْلِكُونَ مِنْهُ خِطَابًا ﴾ means: no one from His creation will be able to start addressing Him, except with His permission. Just as He -the Most High- said:

﴿ مَن ذَا ٱلَّذِى يَشْفَعُ عِندَهُۥٓ إِلَّا بِإِذْنِهِۦ ﴾

[*Sooratul-Baqarah (2): 255*]

[[Meaning: Who [i.e. none] can intercede with Him except by His permission?!]]; and as His -He the Most High's- Saying:

﴿ يَوْمَ يَأْتِ لَا تَكَلَّمُ نَفْسٌ إِلَّا بِإِذْنِهِۦ ﴾

[*Soorah Hood (11): 105*]

[[Meaning: On the Day when the Resurrection comes, no soul will speak except with Allaah's permission.]]"

*AS-SA`DEE: "Meaning: The One Who gives them these great gifts is their Lord and Nurturer: ﴿ رَّبِّ ٱلسَّمَٰوَٰتِ وَٱلْأَرْضِ ﴾: the One who created and controls [the heavens and the earth] ﴿ ٱلرَّحْمَٰنِ ﴾: the One Whose Mercy encompasses everything. So he nurtured them, and had mercy upon them, and was kind and gentle with them, so that they reached the level that they attained.

Then He mentioned His Magnificence and His tremendous Sovereignty on the Day of Resurrection, and that the entire creation will be silent on that Day. They will not speak, and

﴿ لَا يَمْلِكُونَ مِنْهُ خِطَابًا ﴾ [[i.e. they will not be able to address Him]], except for those whom the Most Merciful grants permission to and who speak with that what is correct. So no one will speak unless he fulfils these two conditions: [i] that Allaah permits him to speak, and [ii] that which he says is something correct, because

﴿ ذَٰلِكَ ٱلْيَوْمُ ٱلْحَقُّ ﴾ [[i.e. that is the Day of Truth]]: the Day when falsehood cannot be circulated, and when falsehood will not benefit."

﴿ يَوْمَ يَقُومُ ٱلرُّوحُ وَٱلْمَلَٰٓئِكَةُ صَفًّا لَّا يَتَكَلَّمُونَ إِلَّا مَنْ أَذِنَ لَهُ ٱلرَّحْمَٰنُ وَقَالَ صَوَابًا ﴾ (38)

*AT-TABAREE: "Allaah -the Most High- mentioned about His creation that: On the Day when the *Rooh* and Angels will stand in rows, none of the creation will speak except for those who have been given permission to speak by the Most Merciful: those who say what is correct."

﴿ يَوْمَ يَقُومُ ٱلرُّوحُ ﴾:

*...(`Alee ibn Abee Talhah[1]: from Ibn `Abbaas that he said: "It [i.e. *ar-Rooh*] is an Angel; the greatest Angel of all in size.")

*...Mujaahid[4] said: "It is created beings in the form of the descendants of Aadam: they eat and drink."

*...Qataadah[1] said: "They are descendants of Aadam."

*AS-SAM`AANEE said: "﴿ يَوْمَ يَقُومُ ٱلرُّوحُ ﴾: Mujaahid said: The *Rooh* are created beings resembling the descendants of Aadam, but they are not from the descendants of Aadam; and it is said: it is Jibreel -`*alaihis-Salaam*; and it is said: they are beings created by Allaah, and apart from the Throne there is no creation greater than

يَقُومُ
he/it will stand
from قَامَ

رُوحٌ
spirit, soul, life...

مَلائِكَةٌ
plural of مَلَكٌ
Angel

صَفٌّ
a row, rank

يَتَكَلَّمُونَ
they (will) speak
from تَكَلَّمَ
V root of كَلَمَ

أَذِنَ
he gave permission

قَال
he said

صَوَابٌ
that which is correct

them, and on the Day of Resurrection they will stand in one row and all the Angels in another row. It is also said that ﴿ صَفًّا ﴾ means: in rows..."

*IBN KATHEER: "The people of tafseer disagree as to what is meant by the *Rooh* here, having different sayings:
(firstly): what al-`Awfee* reports from Ibn `Abbaas: that they are the spirits of the descendants of Aadam;
(secondly): that they are descendants of Aadam: this was said by al-Hasan and Qataadah; ...
(thirdly): that they are beings created by Allaah in the form of the descendants of Aadam; and they are neither Angels nor humans, and they eat and drink. This was the saying of Ibn `Abbaas, Mujaahid, Aboo Saalih and al-A`mash.
(fourthly): that it is Jibreel. This was the saying of ash-Sha`bee, Sa`eed ibn Jubayr and ad-Dahhaak, and this saying is witnessed to by the Saying of Allaah -the Mighty and Majestic:

﴿ نَزَلَ بِهِ ٱلرُّوحُ ٱلْأَمِينُ عَلَىٰ قَلْبِكَ لِتَكُونَ مِنَ ٱلْمُنذِرِينَ ﴾

[*Sooratush-Shu`araa· (26): 193-194*]

[[Meaning: Allaah sent Jibreel (*ar-Roohul-Ameen*) down with the Qur·aan. So he recited it to you, O Muhammad, so that your heart retained it; in order that you should be from the Messengers of Allaah who were sent to warn their people.]]

And Muqaatil ibn Hayyaan said: "The *Rooh* here is the noblest of the Angels, the one closest to the Lord -the Mighty and Majestic- and the deliverer of the Revelation.
(fifthly): that it is the Qur·aan, which was said by Ibn Zayd, just like His Saying:

﴿ وَكَذَٰلِكَ أَوْحَيْنَآ إِلَيْكَ رُوحًا مِّنْ أَمْرِنَا ﴾

[*Sooratush-Shooraa (42): 52*]

*He is `Atiyyah ibn Sa`d al-`Awfee, a well known weak narrator from the Taabi`een: 'Taqreebut-Tahdheeb', 'al-Kaashif'.

[[Meaning: And just as We sent Revelation to the rest of Our Messengers We sent this Qur·aan as Revelation by Our command to you, O Muhammad]]; and
(sixthly): that it is an Angel as huge as the rest of the creation put together. `Alee ibn Abee Talhah reported from Ibn `Abbaas that he said: ﴿ يَوْمَ يَقُومُ ٱلرُّوحُ ﴾: "It is a tremendous Angel, from the greatest of the Angels in size."…

And Ibn Jareer [at-Tabaree] withheld, and did not single out a single one of these sayings as being what is correct; and what is most probably correct, and Allaah knows best, is that they are the descendants of Aadam."

*AT-TABAREE: "And what is correct is to say that Allaah -the Most High- informed that His creation will not be capable of addressing Him on the Day when the *Rooh* stands up; and the *Rooh* is a creation from His creation. So it is possible that it is one of the things that we have mentioned, but Allaah knows best which one it is. So there is no narration which would necessitate our submitting to it, nor any proof that any one of these is the right meaning, to the exclusion of the rest; and ignorance of this will not cause any harm."

*Shaikh Ibn `Uthaymeen said in his 'Tafseer Juz· `Amma':

"﴿ ٱلرُّوحُ ﴾: It is Jibreel."

*Shaikh `Atiyyah Muhammad Saalim, said in his completion of Shaikh ash-Shanqeetee's 'Adwaa· ul-Bayaan':
"What the Qur·aan witnesses to, in textual statements similar to this, is that it is Jibreel, *`alaihis-Salaam*, as occurs in the Saying of Allaah -the Most High:

﴿ تَنَزَّلُ ٱلْمَلَـٰٓئِكَةُ وَٱلرُّوحُ فِيهَا بِإِذْنِ رَبِّهِم مِّن كُلِّ أَمْرٍ ﴾

[*Sooratul-Qadr (97): 4*]

[[Meaning: The Angels and Jibreel (*ar-Rooh*) along with them, descend on the Night of Decree (*Laylatul-Qadr*) by the permission of their Lord, with everything decreed by Allaah for the following year]].

So the Angels are joined by the conjunction to the *Rooh* and this is a case of joining the general category along with the specific example; whereas in Sooratul-Qadr the specific follows and is joined to the general, and Allaah -the Most High- knows best."

Muslim reported in his 'Saheeh' (no. 487): "Aboo Bakr ibn Abee Shaybah narrated to us: Muhammad ibn Bishr al-`Abdee narrated to us: Sa`eed ibn Abee `Aroobah narrated to us: from Qataadah: from Mutarrif ibn `Abdullaah ibn ash-Shikhkheer: that `Aa·ishah informed him that Allaah's Messenger (ﷺ), used to say in his *rukoo` and his *sujood*:
<< O venerated One, free of all imperfections (Subbooh), O Blessed and Pure One (Quddoos), Lord of the Angels and the *Rooh* >>."

●

: ﴿لَّا يَتَكَلَّمُونَ إِلَّا مَنْ أَذِنَ لَهُ ٱلرَّحْمَٰنُ وَقَالَ صَوَابًا﴾

*...Mujaahid[1][2] said: "﴿وَقَالَ صَوَابًا﴾: Who spoke the truth in the world and acted upon it."

*...(`Alee ibn Abee Talhah[1] said: Ibn `Abbaas said: "Except one whom the Lord permits because of his testification that none has the right to be worshipped except Allaah: and that is the limit of correctness.")

*IBN KATHEER: "It is like His Saying:

﴿يَوْمَ يَأْتِ لَا تَكَلَّمُ نَفْسٌ إِلَّا بِإِذْنِهِۦ﴾

[*Soorah Hood (11): 105*]

[[Meaning: On the Day when the Resurrection comes, no soul shall speak except with Allaah's permission]];
and as is established in the 'Saheeh' of al-Bukhaaree (no. 806)]:
<< No one will speak on that Day except for the Messengers. >>"

*ASH-SHAWKAANEE: "Meaning: No one will intercede for anyone except for those whom the Most Merciful has permitted to intercede; or: no one will speak except regarding one about whom Allaah has permitted speech, ﴿ وَ ﴾ [[and]] that person is from those who: ﴿ قَالَ صَوَابًا ﴾ [[spoke correctly]]: ad-Dahhaak and Mujaahid said: ﴿ صَوَابًا ﴾ meaning: "with the truth"; and Aboo Saalih said: "(who said): 'Laa ilaaha illallaah' [none has the right to be worshipped except Allaah]." And *sawaab* in origin means: correctness in sayings and actions."

*AT-TABAREE: "...others say: ﴿ إِلَّا مَنْ أَذِنَ لَهُ ٱلرَّحْمَٰنُ ﴾ [[except those given permission to speak by the Most Merciful]]: because of their *Tawheed*; ﴿ وَقَالَ صَوَابًا ﴾ [[and who spoke the truth]]: in the worldly life and worshipped Allaah alone."

*Ibnul-Jawzee said in 'Zaadul-Maseer': "﴿ لَّا يَتَكَلَّمُونَ ﴾: [[they will not speak]]: meaning: the whole of the creation ﴿ إِلَّا مَنْ أَذِنَ لَهُ ٱلرَّحْمَٰنُ ﴾ [[except those whom the Most Merciful permits]]: to speak ﴿ وَقَالَ صَوَابًا ﴾ [[and who spoke the truth]]: meaning: spoke correctness in the world; and that means the testification that none has the right to be worshipped except Allaah, in the saying of the majority of the explainers; and Mujaahid said: Who spoke the truth in the world and acted upon it."

*Shaikh `Atiyyah Muhammad Saalim said in his completion of 'Adwaa· ul-Bayaan' of ash-Shanqeetee:

"So the reality is that this shows that on that day no one will have any power or authority to help anyone, not even with a single word, unless he has been granted permission (by Allaah), just as Allaah -the Most High- said:

﴿ لِّمَنِ ٱلْمُلْكُ ٱلْيَوْمَ لِلَّهِ ٱلْوَٰحِدِ ٱلْقَهَّارِ ﴾

[*Soorah-Ghaafir (40): 16*]

[[Meaning: To Whom belongs Sovereignty this Day?! To Allaah, the One, the Irresistible]]."

AS-SA`DEE: "And on that Day: ﴿ يَقُومُ ٱلرُّوحُ ﴾ [[the *Rooh* will stand]], and it is Jibreel, *`alaihis- Salaam, who is the noblest of the Angels, ﴿ وَٱلْمَلَٰٓئِكَةُ ﴾ [[and the Angels]] also, everyone will stand: ﴿ صَفًّا ﴾ [[in rows]] in humble submission to Allaah ﴿ لَّا يَتَكَلَّمُونَ ﴾ [[none of them will speak]] except with what Allaah grants them permission for. So having encouraged and deterred, and having given glad tidings and a warning, He then said: .. (*Aayah 39*)."

﴿ ذَٰلِكَ ٱلْيَوْمُ ٱلْحَقُّ فَمَن شَآءَ ٱتَّخَذَ إِلَىٰ رَبِّهِۦ مَـَٔابًا ﴾

(39)

ذَٰلِكَ	that
يَوْمٌ	a day
حَقٌّ	true, truth
شَاءَ	he wished
اتَّخَذَ	he took, accepted

*AT-TABAREE: "He -the Most High- says:

﴿ ذَٰلِكَ ٱلْيَوْمُ ﴾: [[That Day]]: meaning: The Day of Resurrection, and it is the Day when the *Rooh* and the Angels will stand in rows.

﴿ ٱلْحَقُّ ﴾: He says: Is something true that will occur, there is no doubt about that.

﴿ فَمَن شَآءَ ٱتَّخَذَ إِلَىٰ رَبِّهِۦ مَـَٔابًا ﴾: He says: So whoever from His servants wishes should take a means of return: by believing in that true Day, and by preparing for it, and by acting in a manner that will lead to salvation from its terrors."

*...Qataadah[1] said: "﴿فَمَن شَآءَ ٱتَّخَذَ إِلَىٰ رَبِّهِۦ مَـَٔابًا﴾: They take a means of returning to Allaah by acting in obedience to Him, and doing whatever will draw them closer to Him."

*...Qataadah[1] said: "﴿مَـَٔابًا﴾: A pathway."

*AL-BAGHAWEE: "﴿ذَٰلِكَ ٱلْيَوْمُ ٱلْحَقُّ﴾: That will occur and come about, and it is the Day of Resurrection;

﴿فَمَن شَآءَ ٱتَّخَذَ إِلَىٰ رَبِّهِۦ مَـَٔابًا﴾: A place of return and a path: by obeying Him; meaning: so whoever wishes will return to Allaah upon obedience to Him."

*AS-SAM`AANEE: "Meaning: The Day of Resurrection is the true and certain Day; and the meaning of ﴿ٱلْحَقُّ﴾ here is that it will occur and is inescapable; and His Saying:

﴿فَمَن شَآءَ ٱتَّخَذَ إِلَىٰ رَبِّهِۦ مَـَٔابًا﴾ means: a fine destination, by obedience and worship."

*ASH-SHAWKAANEE: "﴿فَمَن شَآءَ ٱتَّخَذَ إِلَىٰ رَبِّهِۦ مَـَٔابًا﴾: Meaning: A place of return, to which he returns by means of righteous and correct actions; since if he does good deeds it will draw him closer to Allaah, and if he does evil deeds it will distance him from Him."

*AT-TABARAANEE reported in 'al-Mu`jamul-Kabeer' (2/155/no. 1647): "Muhammad ibn `Abdullaah al-Hadramee narrated to us: Muhammad ibn `Abdullaah ibn Yazeed al-Muqri· narrated to us: Sufyaan ibn `Uyainah narrated to us: from Fitr: from Abut-Tufayl: from Aboo Dharr who said: "Allaah's Messenger (ﷺ) left us such that there was no bird flapping its wings in the sky except that he mentioned to us some knowledge about it, and he (ﷺ) said:
<< There remains nothing which will draw you closer to Paradise and take you further away from the Fire except that I have made it clear to you. >>"

VIII root of: أَخَذَ

إِلَى
to, towards

رَبٌّ
Lord, Nurturer

مَئَابٌ
a place of return

[Shaikh al-Albaanee said in as-Saheehah' (no. 1803): Its chain of narration is 'Saheeh', all of its narrators are reliable…"].

*Shaikh `Atiyyah Muhammad Saalim said, in his completion to 'Adwaa· ul-Bayaan' of Shaikh ash-Shanqeetee:

"﴿فَمَن شَآءَ ٱتَّخَذَ إِلَىٰ رَبِّهِۦ مَـَٔابًا﴾: So since this Day is something that will certainly occur, and on that Day the people will go either to the Hell-Fire, which is the destination that lies in wait ready to ensnare the impious transgressors; or to the place of safety and security: to gardens and grapevines; then after this clear explanation then let whoever wishes take a path leading towards his Lord, taking a way that will lead to a destination with his Lord which he is pleased with for himself. So the statement here 'whoever wishes' suggests a choice, however it is not meant as a statement to provide a choice. Rather it is similar to the Saying of Allaah -the Most High:

﴿فَمَن شَآءَ فَلْيُؤْمِن وَمَن شَآءَ فَلْيَكْفُرْ ۚ إِنَّآ أَعْتَدْنَا لِلظَّـٰلِمِينَ نَارًا﴾

[*Sooratul-Kahf (18): 29*]

[[Meaning: Then whoever wills then let him believe, and whoever wills then let him disbelieve, for indeed We have prepared Hell-Fire for the Disbelievers.]]

So it is closer to being a threat, just as it also contains an indication that the person's will has a role to play in the path he takes, and Allaah -the Most High- knows best. And an evidence for its being a threat is what follows it:..."

*Ibnul-Jawzee said in 'Zaadul-Maseer':
"Then Allaah puts fear into the Disbelievers of Makkah, saying:…"

﴿ إِنَّآ أَنذَرۡنَٰكُمۡ عَذَابٗا قَرِيبٗا يَوۡمَ يَنظُرُ ٱلۡمَرۡءُ مَا قَدَّمَتۡ يَدَاهُ وَيَقُولُ ٱلۡكَافِرُ يَٰلَيۡتَنِي كُنتُ تُرَٰبَۢا ﴾ **(40)**

*AT-TABAREE: "He says: We have warned you, O mankind, of punishment that has drawn near to you and come close, and that will be on ﴿ يَوۡمَ يَنظُرُ ٱلۡمَرۡءُ ﴾: [[the Day when the person will look]]: i.e. the Believer ﴿ مَا قَدَّمَتۡ يَدَاهُ ﴾ [[to whatever his hands put forward]] of good, which he earned in the worldly life, or evil which he left behind. So he will hope for Allaah's reward for his righteous actions, and will fear His punishment for his sins… and the Disbeliever will say on that Day, vainly wishing, when he faces the punishment which Allaah has prepared for those who disbelieved in Him: 'Woe to me, would that I were dust,' like the animals that will be turned to dust."

*...al-Hasan[4] said ﴿ يَوۡمَ يَنظُرُ ٱلۡمَرۡءُ مَا قَدَّمَتۡ يَدَاهُ ﴾: "The person who is a Believer: he takes care to avoid minor sins, and he fears major sins."

*...Qataadah[1] said:

﴿ يَوۡمَ يَنظُرُ ٱلۡمَرۡءُ مَا قَدَّمَتۡ يَدَاهُ وَيَقُولُ ٱلۡكَافِرُ يَٰلَيۡتَنِي كُنتُ تُرَٰبَۢا ﴾

"He is the person who is going to destruction, the unrestricted evil-doer who is now hopeless. So what could stop him saying that, when the disgrace of his evil deeds is upon him: he has come to face the Most Merciful, who is angry with him. So he will wish for death that day, whereas in this world nothing had used to be more disagreeable to him than it."

*AT-TABAREE reported, through two chains of narration, from Aboo Hurairah *-radiyallaahu `anhu-* that Allaah's Messenger (ﷺ) said: << Allaah will judge between His creation: the jinn, mankind,

أَنْذَرْنَا
we have warned
from أَنْذَرَ
IV root of: نَذَرَ

عَذَابٌ
punishment, torment

قَرِيبٌ
near, close

يَوْمَ
on the day

يَنْظُرُ
he looks
from نَظَرَ

مَرْءٌ
a person

يَدَا
dual of يَدٌ
a hand

قَدَّمَتْ
it/she put forward
from قَدَّمَ
II root of قَدَمَ

يَقُولُ he says from قَالَ	
كَافِرٌ a Disbeliever	
يَالَيْتَني 'O woe to me'	
كُنْتُ I was from كَانَ	
تُرابٌ dust, earth	

and the animals. So on that Day revenge will be taken for the hornless ram from the horned ram, until when there remains no claim for any animal upon another, Allaah will say: 'Be dust!' So the Disbeliever will then say:

﴿ يَٰلَيۡتَنِي كُنتُ تُرَٰبَۢا ﴾: 'Woe is me! Would that I were dust!' >>

[Shaikh al-Albaanee declared it authentic due to supporting narrations: as-Saheehah' (no. 1966)].

*AL-BAGHAWEE: "﴿ إِنَّآ أَنذَرۡنَٰكُمۡ عَذَابٗا قَرِيبٗا ﴾: Meaning: Punishment in the Hereafter and whatever is coming is close.

﴿ يَوۡمَ يَنظُرُ ٱلۡمَرۡءُ مَا قَدَّمَتۡ يَدَاهُ ﴾: Meaning: On that Day every person will see the deeds he has put forward, precisely written in his record of deeds..."

*IBN KATHEER: "﴿ يَوۡمَ يَنظُرُ ٱلۡمَرۡءُ مَا قَدَّمَتۡ يَدَاهُ ﴾: All of his deeds will be shown to him: the good and the bad, the old and the new; just like the Saying of Allaah -the Most High:

﴿ وَوَجَدُواْ مَا عَمِلُواْ حَاضِرٗا ﴾

[*Sooratul-Kahf (18): 49*]

[[Meaning: And they will find whatever deeds they did in the worldly life recorded in their record]], and like the Saying of Allaah -the Most High:

﴿ يُنَبَّؤُاْ ٱلۡإِنسَٰنُ يَوۡمَئِذِۭ بِمَا قَدَّمَ وَأَخَّرَ ﴾

[*Sooratul-Qiyaamah (75): 13*]

[[Meaning: On the Day of Resurrection each person will be informed of all the deeds he did]]

﴿ وَيَقُولُ ٱلۡكَافِرُ يَٰلَيۡتَنِي كُنتُ تُرَٰبَۢا ﴾ meaning: On that Day the Disbeliever will wish that in the world he had been dust, and had not been a created being, and had not been brought into existence. This will be when he sees Allaah's punishment and looks at his corrupt deeds, which have been recorded against him by the noble, righteous scribes from the Angels; and it is said that he will wish for this when Allaah judges between the animals which existed in the world. So He will pass judgement justly between them, such that none will be wronged, to the extent that the hornless ram will be avenged upon the horned ram. So when judgement is completed between them He will say to them: 'Be dust!' And they will become dust. So when this happens the Disbeliever will say: ﴿ يَٰلَيۡتَنِي كُنتُ تُرَٰبَۢا ﴾ meaning: 'Would that I were an animal so that I should be returned to being dust.' This meaning occurs in the famous hadeeth of the Horn, and there are reports about that recorded from Aboo Hurairah, `Abdullaah ibn `Amr and others.

This is the end of the Tafseer or Sooratun-Naba·, and all praise and thanks are due to Allaah, and it is He Who guides to and grants attainment of success, and Who protects from error."

*Shaikh `Atiyyah Muhammad Saalim said in his completion of 'Adwaa· ul-Bayaan' of Shaikh ash-Shanqeetee:

"﴿ إِنَّآ أَنذَرۡنَٰكُمۡ عَذَابٗا قَرِيبٗا ﴾ and His Saying:

﴿ يَوۡمَ يَنظُرُ ٱلۡمَرۡءُ مَا قَدَّمَتۡ يَدَاهُ ﴾: All of this is a severe warning, and an emphatic encouragement upon earnest striving to do good, and to seek salvation on the Day of Truth. So we ask Allaah for safety and security.

His Saying: ﴿ يَوۡمَ يَنظُرُ ٱلۡمَرۡءُ مَا قَدَّمَتۡ يَدَاهُ ﴾: So Allaah -the Most High- has clearly explained what the result of this looking will be: either it will be something which pleases him, or otherwise it will terrify him, just as He said:

﴿ يَوۡمَ تَجِدُ كُلُّ نَفۡسٖ مَّا عَمِلَتۡ مِنۡ خَيۡرٖ مُّحۡضَرٗا وَمَا عَمِلَتۡ مِن سُوٓءٖ تَوَدُّ لَوۡ أَنَّ بَيۡنَهَا وَبَيۡنَهُۥٓ أَمَدَۢا بَعِيدٗاۗ وَيُحَذِّرُكُمُ ٱللَّهُ نَفۡسَهُۥۗ وَٱللَّهُ رَءُوفُۢ بِٱلۡعِبَادِ ﴾

[*Soorah Aal-`Imraan (3): 30*]

[[Meaning: On the Day when every person will find whatever good he did presented in full; and whatever evil he did, then he will wish that there were a great distance between him and it; and Allaah warns you of Himself, and Allaah is Compassionate towards His servants]]."

*Shaikh Ibn `Uthaymeen said in his 'Tafseer Juz· `Amma': "﴿ إِنَّآ أَنذَرْنَٰكُمْ عَذَابًا قَرِيبًا ﴾: Meaning: We warn you of a punishment which is close, and it is the Day of Resurrection. So the Day of Resurrection is close, even if the world were to remain for millions of years it would still be close, because:

﴿ كَأَنَّهُمْ يَوْمَ يَرَوْنَهَا لَمْ يَلْبَثُوٓا۟ إِلَّا عَشِيَّةً أَوْ ضُحَىٰهَا ﴾

[*Sooratun-Naazi`aat (79): 46*]

[[Meaning: On the Day when they see that the Hour has been established it will be as if they had not remained in the world except for the evening of a single day, or its morning.]]

So this punishment which Allaah has warned us of is close; there is nothing between the person and it except for his death, and a person does not know when he is going to die. He may enter the morning but not reach the evening, and he may enter the evening but not reach the morning. Therefore it is upon us to be firm in action, and to seize the opportunity before the available time is lost."

*AS-SA`DEE: "﴿ إِنَّآ أَنذَرْنَٰكُمْ عَذَابًا قَرِيبًا ﴾"

[[Meaning: We have warned you of a punishment that is close]]: because it is coming forward quickly, and everything that is coming is close.

﴿ يَوْمَ يَنظُرُ ٱلْمَرْءُ مَا قَدَّمَتْ يَدَاهُ ﴾

[[Meaning: The Day when the person will look to whatever his hands put forward]], meaning: this is what will concern him and alarm him. So therefore let him look to this whilst he is still in this world, just as Allaah -the Most High- said:

﴿ يَٰٓأَيُّهَا ٱلَّذِينَ ءَامَنُوا۟ ٱتَّقُوا۟ ٱللَّهَ وَلْتَنظُرْ نَفْسٌ مَّا قَدَّمَتْ لِغَدٍ ۖ وَٱتَّقُوا۟ ٱللَّهَ ۚ إِنَّ ٱللَّهَ خَبِيرٌۢ بِمَا تَعْمَلُونَ ﴾

[*Sooratul-Hashr (59): 18*]

[[Meaning: O you who believe! Fear, revere, and be dutiful to Allaah, by carrying out whatever He has made obligatory and avoiding committing sins against Him; and let each one of you look to see what deeds he has put forward for the Day of Resurrection: are they righteous deeds that will lead to his salvation, or evil deeds that will cause his destruction? So fear Allaah and be dutiful to Him, for Allaah is fully aware and knows all of your deeds: the good and the evil; nothing from them is hidden from Him, and He will recompense you for all of them]] -the Aayahs.

So if he finds good, then let him praise Allaah; and if he finds other than that, then let him blame no one but himself. So it is because of this that the Disbelievers will wish for death, because of the severity of their despair and regret.

We ask Allaah to keep us safe from Disbelief and all evil; indeed He is the Beneficent, the Most Generous.

The Tafseer of Soorah `Amma· is completed, and all praise is for Allaah, the Lord and Nurturer of the entire creation."

APPENDIX ONE:

BIOGRAPHIES OF THE AUTHORS OF THE BOOKS OF TAFSEER:

*AT-TABAREE:

Muhammad ibn Jareer ibn Yazeed, Aboo Ja`far at-Tabaree: "The imaam, the outstanding scholar, the Mujtahid. The scholar of his time: Aboo Ja`far at-Tabaree, the author of excellent works.

He was from the people of Aamul in Tabaristaan (a town 80 miles NE of Tehran in Persia). He was born in the year 224 H, and began seeking knowledge after the year 240 H. He travelled greatly and met the pre-eminent men. He was singular amongst the people of his time in knowledge, intellect and in the great number of his works. It is rare that anyone the like of him is seen...

Al-Khateeb al-Baghdaadee said of him: 'He gathered such branches of knowledge as were not attained by anyone from the people of his time. He had memorised the Book of Allaah; he was knowledgeable of the different modes of recitation; he had insight of the meaning; he was a learned jurist with regard to the rulings contained in the Qur·aan; he was a scholar of the details of the Sunnah and of its chains of narration; the authentic and the unauthentic; he knew the abrogating texts and the abrogated texts; he was knowledgeable of the sayings of the Companions and the Taabi`een; he was well-acquainted with the past events and history of the peoples, and he compiled the famous book: 'Narratives and history of the nations'; and he compiled his 'Tafseer': the like of which has not been written. He also wrote a book entitled 'Tahdheeb-Aathaar', and I have not seen a similar work the like of it, but he did not complete it. He also wrote many books about the principles and details of Fiqh, and his preferred sayings from the sayings of the jurists. He had certain verdicts specific to him which were preserved'." ['Siyar A`laamin-Nubalaa·' of adh-Dhahabee: (14/267-)].

Concerning his Tafseer (printed in thirty volumes) Aboo Haamid al-Isfaraayeenee said: "If a person were to travel to China to obtain the Tafseer of Muhammad ibn Jareer it would not be too much."

Shaikhul-Islaam Ibn Taimiyyah said: "As for the Tafseers that the people have with them, then the most authentic of them is the Tafseer of Muhammad ibn Jareer at-Tabaree, because he mentions the sayings reported from the Salaf with established chains of narration, and it does not contain innovation, and he does not report from those accused of being liars such as Muqtaatil ibn Bukayr and al-Kalbee."
['Majmoo`ul-Fataawaa':13/385]

Ibn Katheer said, concerning his 'Tafseer': "He authored a complete Tafseer which is such that it has no equal," and concerning him: "He had high standing in worship, *zuhd* (abstaining from the unnecessary things of this world), piety, and establishing the truth: not being prevented from that by the blame of anyone. He had a fine voice in recitation, along with complete knowledge of the modes of recitation - upon the finest characteristics. He was one of the major righteous people, and one of the scholars of hadeeth who gathered in Egypt in the time of Ibn Tooloon; and they were: Muhammad ibn Ishaaq ibn Khuzaymah - the imaam of the imaams, Muhammad ibn Nasr al-Marwazee, Muhammad ibn Haaroon ar-Ruwayaanee, and this one: Muhammad ibn Jareer at-Tabaree..."
['al-Bidaayah wan-Nihaayah' (11/156-)].

Al-Firghaanee said: "Muhammad ibn Jareer was of those who did not care about the blame of anyone for Allaah's sake, along with the very great harm he suffered and the slanders he received from the ignorant, envious and apostates; but as for the people of knowledge and Religion, then they do not deny his knowledge, his abstinence with regard to this world and how he renounced it. He sufficed himself with a small inheritance left for him by his father in Tabaristaan." And al-Firghaanee said: "I heard him say: "My father's inheritance has been delayed, so I had to remove the sleeves of my robe and sell them."
['Tabaqaatush-Shaafi`iyyah': (3/120), quoted in Dr. `Abdullaah at-Turkee's introduction to 'Jaami`ul-Bayaan'.]

It was mentioned about him that everyday for forty years he would fill forty pages with his writing; and that he originally proposed dictating his 'history' of a length of thirty thousand pages, and his Tafseer of similar length, but was dissuaded by his students and so reduced each of them to a tenth of the intended size, saying: "Indeed we belong to Allaah! Peoples' eagerness has died!"

as-Suyootee said in 'al-Itqaan' (2/476): "So if you were to say: 'Which of the tafseers do you direct us towards, and tell a person to rely upon?' Then I say: The tafseer of Aboo Ja`far ibn Jareer at-Tabaree, about which the reputable scholars have agreed that its like has not been written in the field of tafseer. an-Nawawee said in his 'Tahdheeb': 'No one has written the like of the book of Ibn Jareer in tafseer'."

He passed away at the time of Maghrib on the night of the 28th of Shawwal in the year 310 H, at the age of 86 *-rahimahullaah.*

***AS-SAM`AANEE:**

"The imaam, the outstanding scholar, the Muftee of Khuraasaan, Shaikh of the Shaafi`ees; Abul-Muzaffar Mansoor ibn Muhammad ibn `Abdil-Jabbaar ibn Ahmad, at-Tameemee, as-Sam`aanee, al-Marwazee, previously al-Hanafee, then ash-Shaafi`ee.

He was born in the year 426 H...
He went out on foot to perform Hajj at a time when riding parties were prevented from travelling, so he and a group of people were captured by brigands. So he bore this with patience until Allaah freed him from these bedouins, and he performed Hajj and accompanied az-Zanjaanee. He used to relate: < They took us captive, so I used to tend their camels. So it happened that their chief wanted to marry off his daughter, so they said: we will have to travel to a town to find someone to perform the marriage for us. So one of their men said: 'The man who tends our camels is the jurist of Khuraasaan.' So they asked me about some matters, and I answered them, and I spoke to them in correct Arabic, so they became embarrassed and excused themselves. So I performed the marriage for them, and said the (marriage)

address, so they were happy and asked me to accept some reward from that, but I refused. So they conveyed me to Makkah in the middle of the year. >

`Abdul-Ghaafir said in his 'Taareekh': "He was the singular scholar of his age in excellence and behaviour, and in *zuhd* and piety. He came from a household of knowledge and *zuhd*. He acquired knowledge of Fiqh from his father, and he became one of the foremost amongst the people of speculation. He then studied the books of hadeeth, performed Hajj and returned, and abandoned the way upon which he had debated for thirty years and became a Shaafi`ee. He manifested this in the year 468 H and the people of Marw were thrown into turmoil and the common folk became perplexed. So letters were sent concerning him by the Ameer of Balkh which spoke harshly against him. So he left Marw in the company of Dhul-Majdayn Abul-Qaasim al-Moosawee and a group of students, and he was attended to by a number of the jurists. So he went to Toos, and proceeded on to Naysaaboor. So he was met by the students with a great reception in the time of Nizaamul-Mulk, and `Ameedul-Hadrah Aboo Sa`d. So they honoured him and gave him a position of great respect, and a gathering for admonition was established for him in the Shaafi`ee school; and he was an ocean with regard to admonition and he was a great memorizer, so he was greatly accepted by the people. He attained firmness and prominence in the Shaafi`ee madhhab and then he returned to Marw and taught there in the Shaafi`ee school, and an-Nizaam gave him precedence over his peers, and his students became apparent. Then he went off to Asbahaan in a state of high standing.

He wrote the book 'al-Istilaam,' and the book 'al-Burhaan,' and 'al-Amaalee' in Hadeeth, and he stood firmly with the people of the Hadeeth, the Sunnah and the Jamaa`ah; and he was a thorn in the eyes of the opponents, and a proof for the people of the Sunnah.

[His grandson] Aboo Sa`d said: 'My grandfather wrote a work of Tafseer, and in Fiqh, Usool and Hadeeth. His Tafseer is of three volumes' …

The Imaam Aboo `Alee ibn as-Saffaar said: 'When I debate with Abul-Muzaffar then it is as if I am debating with an imaam from the Taabi`een, because of the signs of the righteous people which I see in him.'

He also said about himself: "I never forgot anything which I had memorized."

... He died in the year 489 H, having lived for sixty-three years - *rahimahullaah*." ['Siyar A`laamin-Nubalaa·' (19/114-119)]

Ibn al-`Imaad said about him in 'Shadharaatudh-Dhahab' (3/393): "The imaam, the eminent scholar, Abul-Muzaffar as-Sam`aanee Mansoor ibn Muhammad, at-Tameemee, al-Marwazee, al-Hanafee, then ash-Shaafi`ee. He learned Fiqh from this father and from others, and he was the imaam of his age in the madhhab of Aboo Haneefah. But when he performed Hajj, that which necessitated his moving to the madhhab of ash-Shaafi`ee became clear to him in al-Hijaaz. So when he returned to Marw he suffered great harm because of his changing over. He wrote many books regarding the Shaafi`ee madhhab and he wrote in refutation of the opponents, and he wrote 'at-Tabaqaat' which he excelled in, and he wrote a good and fine Tafseer..." *-rahimahullaah.*

***AL-BAGHAWEE:**

"Shaikhul-Islaam, the outstanding exemplary scholar, the Haafiz: Shaikhul-Islaam, the reviver of the Sunnah, Aboo Muhammad al-Husayn ibn Mas`ood ibn Muhammad ibn al-Farraa·, al-Baghawee, ash-Shaafi`ee: the scholar of Tafseer; the compiler of works such as 'Sharhus-Sunnah,' 'Ma`aalimut-Tanzeel,' 'al-Masaabeeh' and the book 'at-Tahdheeb' upon the madhhab, and 'al-Jam`u baynas-Saheehayn,' and 'al-Arba`eena hadeethan' and other works.

He acquired knowledge of Fiqh from the Shaikh of the Shaafi`ees al-Qaadee Husayn ibn Muhammad al-Marwaroodhee, the author of 'at-Ta`leeqah,' before the year 460 H....

Al-Baghawee was given the title 'Muhiyyus-Sunnah' (the reviver of the Sunnah), and the 'the pillar of the Religion', and he was a person of nobility and an Imaam. He was a person of knowledge and outstanding scholar. He abstained from the superfluous things of this world and was satisfied with a

little. He used to eat dry bread on its own, but was criticised by people for that, so he began accompanying it with oil. His father used to make and sell fur garments (al-Farraa·). He was granted blessing in his writings, and granted complete acceptance with regard to them: this was on account of his fine resolve, and true and sincere intention. The scholars vied in acquiring his works, and he would not deliver a lesson except in a state of purification. He was moderate in his dress: he wore a crude robe, and a small turban - upon the way of the Salaf- which he wore and tied as they did. He was firmly established in Tafseer, and fully proficient in Fiqh -may Allaah have mercy upon him…"
['Siyar A`laamin-Nubalaa·' of adh-Dhahabee: (19/439-)]

He was born in the town of Bagh (30 miles NW of Herat in Afghanistan) in Khuraasaan, and travelled throughout Khuraasaan seeking knowledge, finally settling in Marw ar-Roodh (SE Turkmenistan) where he taught and compiled his works, and died in the year of 516 H at over eighty years of age.

Ibn Katheer said: "…He excelled in the branches of knowledge, and he was the foremost scholar of his time in them. He adhered to the Religion, was pious, a 'zaahid,' and a righteous worshipper." *rahimahullaah.*
['al-Bidaayah wan-Nihaayah (12/206).']

***IBN KATHEER:**

"He is Abul-Fidaa·, `Imaadud-Deen, Ismaa`eel ibn (ash-Shaikh Abee Hafs Shihaabud-Deen) `Umar - who was the 'khateeb of his village - ibn Katheer ibn Daw· ibn Katheer ibn Zar' al-Qurashee, al-Basrawee in origin, ad-Dimashqee with regard to his upbringing, nurturing and education. He was born in the town of Mijdal, in the district of the town of Busraa, to the [north-] east of Damascus, in the year of 701 H, and his father was a khateeb. His father died when he was four years old, so he was brought up by his brother, the Shaikh `Abdul-Wahhaab, and he learned Fiqh from him at the beginning of his affair.

Then he moved to Damascus in the year 706 H, at the age of five. He then acquired knowledge of Fiqh from Shaikh Burhaanuddeen Ibraaheem ibn

`Abdur-Rahmaan al-Fazaaree, well known as Ibn al-Firkaah - who died in the year 729 H.

He also heard in Damascus from `Eesaa ibn al-Muta``im, and from Ahmad ibn Abee Taalib - who lived more than a hundred years and who was well known as Ibnush-Shihnah, and also known as al-Hajjaar -who died in year 730 H. Also from al-Qaasim ibn `Asaakir, and Ibnush-Sheeraazee, Ishaaq ibn al-Aamidee, and Muhammad ibn Zarraad. He closely accompanied the Shaikh Jamaaluddeen Yoosuf ibn az-Zakiyy al-Mizzee - the author of 'Tahdheebul-Kamaal' and 'Atraaful-Kutubis-Sittah' who died in the year 742 H; and he greatly benefited from him and became proficient in knowledge, and he married his daughter.

He also studied a great deal with Shaikhul-Islaam Taqiyyuddeen Ibn Taimiyyah, who died in the year 728 H. He closely accompanied him, loved him and benefited from his knowledge. He also studied with the Shaikh, the Haafiz, the historian Shamsuddeen adh-Dhahabee Muhammad ibn Ahmad ibn Qaaymaaz, who died in the year 748 H.

He was granted 'ijaazah' (permission to narrate) in Egypt by Aboo Moosaa al-Qaraafee, and al-Husaynee, and `Alee ibn `Umar al-Waanee, Yoosuf al-Hutanee and others.

Al-Haafiz Shamsuddeen adh-Dhahabee said of him in 'al-Mu`jamul-Mukhtass': "The imaam, the muftee, the outstanding muhaddith, the precise jurist, the critical and precise scholar of tafseer. He has a number of beneficial works."

Al-Haafiz Ibn Hajr said of him in 'ad-Durarul-Kaaminah': "He became occupied with hadeeth, carefully studying its texts and narrators. He could quote a great deal from memory and was delightful in speech. His works spread widely in his lifetime, and people benefited from them after his death. He was not upon the way of those muhadditheen who merely seek briefer chains of narration, and seek to distinguish shorter from longer chains of narration and other such disciplines of theirs; rather he was from the jurists of the muhadditheen.'…"

"His works included:

(1) 'Tafseerul-Qur·aanil-Kareem,' and it was one of the most beneficial books of tafseer based upon narrations. He would explain the Qur·aan with the Qur·aan, and then with the famous ahaadeeth from the dependable sources of the muhadditheen - along with their chains of narration. He discussed the chains of narration with the terms of rejection and acceptance, and made clear anything the narrations contained with regard to strangeness, being contrary to what is authentic, or confliction with the reliable reports. Then he would mention the reported sayings from the Companions and the Taabi`een.
As-Suyootee said: "The like of it, similar in form, has not been written."

(2) His history entitled 'al-Bidaayah wan-Nihaayah,' in which he mentioned the stories of the Prophets and the previous nations, based upon what occurs in the Noble Qur·aan and the authentic narrations…then he carefully detailed the Prophetic Seerah, and the history of Islaam to his time. Then he went on to mention the tribulations, signs of the Last Hour, the forthcoming battles and the conditions in the Hereafter….

He died on Thursday, the 26th of Sha`baan in the year 774 H, at the age of 74; and al-Haafiz Ibn Hajr said: He lost his eyesight at the end of his life - *rahimahullaah wa radiyallaahu `anhu.*"
[Taken from the introduction to 'al-Baa`ithul-Hatheeth'; the biography was compiled by Shaikh Muhammad `Abdur-Razzaaq Hamzah.]

Ibn al-`Imaad said in 'Shadharaatudh-Dhahab' (6/231/232): "…He had many students; from them was Ibn Hajjee who said about him: 'He was the greatest memorizer of the texts of hadeeth that we have come across, and the one best acquainted with their defects, and their narrators, and the authentic and the unauthentic from them, and his peers and his Shaikhs acknowledged that for him. I do not think, despite the frequency with which I went to him, that I ever met him except I took benefit from him.' Others, as Qaadee Shahbah mentioned in his 'Tabaqaat' stated that he was a particularly close student of Ibn Taimiyyah, and used to defend him and follow many of his views; and he used to give verdict with his view regarding divorce, and he was put to trial because of it and suffered harm. He died in Sha`baan, and was buried…next to his Shaikh, Ibn Taimiyyah." -*rahimahullaah.*

***ASH-SHAWKAANEE:**

Muhammad ibn `Alee ibn Muhammad ibn `Abdullaah, ash-Shawkaanee, then as-San`aanee [the capital of Yemen]. He was born on Monday the 28th of Dhul-Qa`dah in 1173 H in the town of Hijrah Shawkaan.

He grew up in the manner of students of legislated knowledge, memorizing the Qur·aan and becoming proficient in it, and he memorized many of the texts before he began serious study by the age of ten. Then he sat with the major Shaikhs, and he greatly occupied himself with studying history in the sciences of the language. His father did not allow him to occupy himself with other than knowledge, nor to leave San`aa. He sat to deliver verdicts at the age of twenty, and he had thirteen lessons each day: some he delivered, and others he studied with his Shaikhs.
['al-Badrut-Taali`': (2/215, 218-219)]

He authored 278 works, including works of Tafseer, Fiqh, Usoolul-Fiqh, the `Aqeedah of the Salaf, and in refutation of blind-following (taqleed).

al-`Allaamah Hasan ibn Ahmad al-Bahkalee said...: (start of quote): "In the year 1250 H, in the month of Jumaadal-Aakhirah, our Shaikh Muhammad ibn `Alee ash-Shawkaanee passed away. He was the judge of the whole community, Shaikhul-Islaam, the verifier, the `Allaamah, the imaam, sultaan of the scholars, imaam of the world....

So in summary, he did not see anyone the like of himself; nor did he see anyone who had seen the like of him in knowledge, piety and establishment of the truth with strength of spirit and eloquence of tongue....
He was born on Monday, the 28th of the sacred month of Dhul-Qa`dah in the year 1172 H....

He studied under his father, and studied continuously under the Qaadee, imaam of the details of Fiqh in his time Ahmad ibn Muhammad al-Haraazee, and he derived benefit from him in Fiqh... He learned Arabic grammar and morphology from as-Sayyid al-`Allaamah Ismaa`eel ibn Hasan, and al-`Allaamah `Abdullaah ibn Ismaa`eel an-Nahmee, and al-`Allaamah al-Qaasim ibn Muhammad al-Khawlaanee... and in many of the branches of knowledge he studied constantly with the reviver of his time as-

Sayyid `Abdul-Qaadir ibn Ahmad al-Kawkabaanee; and in the science of hadeeth he took from al-Haafiz `Alee ibn Ibraaheem ibn `Aamir, and from other Shaikhs besides them....

He authored magnificent, delightful, beneficial, and useful works in most branches of knowledge; from them 'Naylul-Awtaar' - a commentary upon 'Muntaqal-Akhbaar' of [Majduddeen `Abdus-Salaam] Ibn Taimiyyah - *rahimahullaah*- in four volumes the like of which is not to be seen in these times with regard to its careful verification and precision. He gave each matter its due right, with justice and fairness; and did not adhere to blind-following. He quoted the positions of the later scholars and of the Predecessors. His noble Shaikhs and other prominent scholars related it from him, and it spread throughout the lands in his lifetime. It was read to him many times, and the scholars derived benefit from it; and it was the only one out of his works that he was personally satisfied with, because of its high level of accuracy, and its close adherence to proof in the best manner. He wrote it during the lifetime of his Shaikhs, and they were able to point out certain points, which he edited.

He also wrote the large Tafseer entitled 'Fathul-Qadeer' which combined the sciences of narration of hadeeth, and its understanding... ...

And I [i.e. his student Hasan ibn Ahmad al-Bahkalee] learned from him in many of the fields of knowledge, and I took from him most of his noble works, and with his death the shining lamp of Yemen was extinguished for them; and I do not think that in precision and verification they will see the like of him." (end of quote.)

And the Lord of creation, the One free of all imperfections-blessed this Qaadee and Imaam from the vast ocean of His Generosity with three things which I do not know to have been combined in these later times for anyone besides him: Firstly: Vast and deep knowledge of all the different branches, types and forms of knowledge; secondly: the great number of students he had who were verifiers, people of nobility and precision: people of discerning intellect, and outstanding virtues...; thirdly: the great number of his skilled and precise works, and his intricate treatises and responses which in their number outstripped great scholars, and whose precision and exactness reached every possible limit..."-*rahimahullaah*.

['at-Taajul-Mukallal' (pp.452-461) of `Allaamah Siddeeq Hasan Khaan al-Qanoojee; and the introduction to 'Fathul-Qadeer.']

*AS-SA`DEE:

"Ash-Shaikh Aboo `Abdillaah `Abdur-Rahmaan ibn Naasir ibn `Abdillaah ibn Naasir Aal-Sa`dee, from the tribe of Tameem. He was born in the town of `Unayzah in the district of al-Qaseem [Saudi Arabia], on the 12th of Muharram 1307 H and his mother died when he was four years old. Then his father died when he was seven years old, so he grew up as an orphan. However he had a fine up bringing and it was noticed that from an early age he was distinguished by intelligence and a desire to learn. He read the whole Qur·aan after the death of his father and then memorized it completely, and he was fully proficient in it at the age of eleven. Then he occupied himself with acquiring knowledge from the scholars of his land, and from those who came to his land. So he strove and exerted himself until he acquired a good portion of every branch of knowledge. Upon reaching the age of twenty-three he sat to teach. So he would learn and also teach, and spend all of his time in that. This continued until the year 1350 H, when he took charge of all teaching in his town, and all students referred back to him.

He took knowledge from Shaikh Ibraaheem ibn Hamd ibn Jaasir, and he was the first teacher he studied with. He described his Shaikh as a memorizer of hadeeth, and he would speak about his piety and how he used to love and take care of the poor. Often a poor person would come to him in winter and he would take off one of his two garments and give it to the poor person, even though he himself needed it and possessed very little himself - *rahimahullaah.*

Also from his Shaikhs was Muhammad ibn `Abdul-Kareem ash-Shibl, with whom he learned Fiqh, sciences of Arabic language and other than that.

He also studied with ash-Shaikh Saalih ibn `Uthmaan al-Qaadee, the judge of `Unayzah. He learnt from him Tawheed, Tafseer, Fiqh: its Usool and its details, and the sciences of the Arabic language. He was the one whom he studied with the most, and he kept his company constantly until he passed away -*rahimahullaah*.

He also studied with Shaikh `Abdullaah ibn `Aayid, and Shaikh Sa`b al-Quwayjaree, and Shaikh `Alee as-Sinaanee, and Shaikh `Alee an-Naasir Aboo Waadee with whom he studied hadeeth, and took the six books and others from him with 'ijaazah' (permission to narrate).

He also studied with Shaikh Muhammad ibn ash-Shaikh `Abdul-`Azeez Aal Muhammad al-Maani` (the director of cultural/educational affairs in the Kingdom of Saudi Arabia at present); he studied with him in `Unayzah.

Also from his Shaikhs was Shaikh Muhammad ash-Shanqeetee (who settled in the Hijaaz...) when he came to teach in `Unayzah. He studied with him Tafseer, Hadeeth, the sciences of Hadeeth, and the sciences of the language - such as grammar, morphology and so on.

He was upon a high level of virtuous manners, showing humility with the young and the old, and the rich and the poor. He used to spend some of his time sitting in gatherings with whoever wished to attend, so the gathering would be a gathering of knowledge. He was keen that these gatherings should discuss matters of knowledge and social affairs, and the people of the gatherings would derive great benefit from the useful discussions they involved themselves in. So their recreational gatherings were turned into gatherings of worship and knowledge. He would speak to each person with whatever befitted him, and would discuss with him matters that would be beneficial to his worldly life and his Hereafter.

He would frequently resolve dispute in a just manner which satisfied both sides.

He had great concern for the poor, the needy, and strangers and he would personally assist them as far as he was able, and he would encourage the wealthy people - those whom he knew to love doing good - to be compassionate towards them.

He was upon a very high level of good manners, chastity, purity of spirit, and firmly resolved and serious in all his affairs.

He was also the best of people in his manner of teaching, and the best at causing his students to understand…

He occupied himself most of all and benefited most from the books of Shaikhul-Islaam Ibn Taimiyyah and his student Ibnul-Qayyim. This benefited him greatly with regard to knowledge of Usool, Tawheed, Tafseer, and Fiqh and other branches of beneficial knowledge…

He was especially proficient in Tafseer, having read a number of Tafseers and excelling in it. He authored a fine Tafseer, in a number of volumes…entitled 'Tayseerul-Kareemir-Rahmaan fee Tafseer Kalaamil-Mannaan'….

He passed away at the age of 69 in the year 1376 in the town of `Unayzah - *rahimahullaah…*"

[Abridged from the biography written by one of his students and included as a preface to his Tafseer].

APPENDIX TWO:

CHAINS OF NARRATION FOR THE REPORTS FROM THE SALAF:

`Abdullaah ibn `Amr *-radiyallaahu `anhumaa*:

[1] at-Tabaree –Muhammad ibn Bashshaar ['Bundaar': *thiqah..*] –Muhammad ibn Ibraaheem ibn `Adiyy [*thiqah*] –Sa`eed ibn Abee `Aroobah: *thiqah haafiz*] – Qataadah [ibn Di`aamah: *thiqah haafiz...*] -Aboo Ayyoob al-Azdee [al-Muraaghee: *thiqah n .nath-thaalithah, yarwee `an Ibn `Amr*] – `Abdullaah ibn `Amr.

Aboo Hurairah *-radiyallaahu `anhu*:

[1] at-Tabaree- Tameem ibn al-Muntasir [*thiqah*] – Ishaaq ibn Yoosuf [al-Waasitee, al-Azraq: *thiqah*] – Shareek [ibn `Abdillaah al-Qaadee: *sadooq yukhti· katheeran.* Ibn Hibbaan mentioned that the narrators of Waasit narrated from him before his senility] – `Aasim ibn Abin-Nujood [al-Koofee, al-Muqri·: *sadooq lahu awhaam*] – Aboo Saalih Dhakwaan [*thiqah thabt*] – Aboo Hurairah.

Mujaahid:

[1] at-Tabaree –Muhammad ibn `Amr [Aboo Bakr al-Baahilee, al-Basree: *thiqah*] –Aboo `Aasim [ad-Dahhaak ibn Makhlad: *thiqah thabt*] –`Eesaa [ibn Maymoon al-Jurashee: *thiqah*] –Ibn Abee Najeeh [`Abdullaah ibn Yasaar: *thiqah*] –Mujaahid.*

*[This chain of narration was declared 'Saheeh' by Shaikh Muqbil ibn Haadee al-Waadi`ee -*rahimahullaah-* in his verification of 'Tafseer Ibn Katheer' (2/443); and he described the narrations of Ibn Abee Najeeh from Mujaahid as being acceptable narrations, by way of a manuscript which al-Qaasim ibn Abee Bazzah had from Mujaahid (ibid 2/451).

Shaikhul-Islaam Ibn Taimiyyah *-rahimahullaah-* said: '' As for the saying that the narrations of Ibn Abee Najeeh from Mujaahid are not authentic, then the response is that the tafseer of Ibn Abee Najeeh from Mujaahid is from the most authentic tafseers...'' ('Majmoo`ul-Fataawaa': 17/408-409)]

[2] at-Tabaree –al-Haarith [ibn Muhammad ibn Abee Usaamah, at-Tameemee: *thiqah*] –al-Hasan [ibn Moosaa al-Ashyab: *thiqah*] –Warqaa·
[ibn `Umar al-Yashkuree: *thiqah*] –Ibn Abee Najeeh – Mujaahid.

[3] at-Tabaree –Muhammad ibn al-Muthannaa [*thiqah hujjah haafiz*] – Muhammad ibn Ibraaheem ibn `Adiyy [*thiqah*] –Shu`bah [ibn al-Hajjaaj: *thiqah haafiz mutqin, Ameerul-Mu·mineen fil-Hadeeth*] – Mansoor [ibn al-Mu`tamir: *thiqah haafiz mutqin*] –Mujaahid.

[4] at-Tabaree –Muhammad ibn Bashshaar ['Bundaar': *thiqah..*]- Aboo `Aamir [`Abdul-Malik ibn `Amr al-`Aqadee: *thiqah*] –Sufyaan [ibn Sa`eed ibn Masrooq ath-Thawree: *haafiz hujjah mutqin thabt ]* –Ibn Abee Najeeh [`Abdullaah ibn Yasaar: *thiqah..*] –Mujaahid.
[9] at-Tabaree –Ibn Bashshaar [Muhammad, 'Bundaar': *imaam haafiz thiqah thabt..*] –`Abdur-Rahmaan [ibn Mahdee: *imaam haafiz naaqid mutqin hujjah thabt*] –Sufyaan [ibn Sa`eed ibn Masrooq ath-Thawree: *haafiz hujjah mutqin thabt*] – Mansoor [ibn al-Mu`tamir: *thiqah haafiz mutqin*] – Mujaahid.

Qataadah:

[1] at-Tabaree –Bishr [ibn Mu`aadh al-`Aqadee: *sadooq*] –Yazeed ibn Zurai` [*imaam hujjah haafiz mutqin thabt*] –Sa`eed ibn Abee `Aroobah [al-Yashkuree: *thiqah haafiz...*] –Qataadah.*

*[This chain of narration was declared 'Saheeh' by Shaikh Muqbil in his verification of 'Tafseer Ibn Katheer' (2/417).]

[2] at-Tabaree –Muhammad ibn `Abdil-A`laa [as-San`aanee: *thiqah*] - Muhammad ibn Thawr [as-San`aanee: *thiqah*] –Ma`mar [ibn Raashid: *thiqah thabt...*] – Qataadah.

[3] at-Tabaree – Ya`qoob [ibn Ibraaheem ad-Dawraqee, al-Haafiz: *thiqah*] –Ibn `Ulayyah [Ismaa`eel ibn Ibraaheem ibn Miqsam: *thiqah hujjah haafiz*] –Sa`eed ibn Abee `Aroobah [*thiqah haafiz*] – Qataadah.

Al-Hasan al-Basree:

[1] at-Tabaree –Ya`qoob [ibn Ibraaheem ad-Dawraqee, al-Haafiz: *thiqah*] – Ibn `Ulayyah [Ismaa`eel ibn Ibraaheem ibn Miqsam: *thiqah hujjah haafiz*] – Aboo Rajaa· [Muhammad ibn Sayf al-Huddaanee: *taabi`ee thiqah*] – al-Hasan.*

*[This chain of narration was declared 'Saheeh' by Shaikh Muqbil in his verification of 'Tafseer Ibn Katheer' (2/551).]

[2] at-Tabaree –Zakariyyaa ibn Yahyaa ibn Abee Zaa·idah [*sadooq*] -Muslim ibn Ibraaheem al-Azdee [*thiqah*] – `Abdullaah ibn Bakr ibn `Abdillaah al-Maazinee [*sadooq*] – al-Hasan.

[4] at-Tabaree –Aboo Kurayb [Muhammad ibn al-`Alaa·: *thiqah haafiz*] – Wakee` [ibn al-Jarraah: *thiqah haafiz thaabit*] – Mubaarak [ibn Fadaalah: *sadooq, laakinnahu mudallis...minas-saadisah*] – al-Hasan.

Sufyaan ath-Thawree:

[1] at-Tabaree – Ibn Bashshaar [Muhammad, 'Bundaar': *thiqah...*] and Muhammad ibn al-Muthannaa [*thiqah thabt*] = `Abdur-Rahmaan [ibn Mahdee: *thiqah thabt haafiz*] – Sufyaan [ath-Thawree: *thiqah haafiz...*] – Mansoor [ibn al-Mu`tamir: *thiqah thabt*] – Ibraaheem an-Nakha`ee.

[2] at-Tabaree – Ibn Bashshaar ['Bundaar': *imaam haafiz thiqah thabt..*]-
`Abdur-Rahmaan [ibn Mahdee: *imaam haafiz naaqid...*] – Sufyaan.

Aboo Razeen (Mas`ood ibn Maalik al-Asadee):

[1] at-Tabaree – Ibn Bashshaar [Muhammad,'Bundaar': thiqah…] and Muhammad ibn al-Muthannaa [*thiqah thabt*] = `Abdur-Rahmaan [ibn Mahdee: *thiqah thabt haafiz*] – Sufyaan [ath-Thawree: *thiqah haafiz…*] – Mansoor [ibn al-Mu'tamir: *thiqah thabt*] – Aboo Razeen.

Ibn Zayd (`Abdur-Rahmaan ibn Zayd ibn Aslam):

[1] at-Tabaree – Yoonus [ibn `Abdil-A`laa as-Sadafee: thiqah] – Ibn Wahb [`Abdullaah ibn Wahb ibn Muslim: thiqah haafiz `aabid] – Ibn Zayd.

**[`Alee ibn Abee Talhah** (from Ibn `Abbaas *-radiyallaahu `anhumaa-*):

[1] at-Tabaree – `Alee [ibn 'Abdir-Rahmaan ibn Muhammad al-Makhzoomee: *sadooq*] – Aboo Saalih [`Abdullaah ibn Saalih ibn Muhammad ibn Muslim, al-Misree, the scribe of al-Layth ibn Sa`d: *sadooq katheerul-ghalat, thabata fee kitaabihi..*] – Mu`aawiyah [ibn Saalih ibn Hudayr: Qaadee of al-Andalus: *sadooq lahu awhaam*] – `Alee ibn Abee Talhah [`Alee ibn Saalim ibn al-Makhaariq al-Haashimee: *sadooq qad yukhti., yursilu. Arsala 'an Ibn `Abbaas wa lam yarahu*]-..-(from Ibn `Abbaas *-radiyallaahu `anhumaa.*)] *

* The narrations of `Alee ibn Abee Talhah from Ibn `Abbaas are numerous in the 'Tafseer' of at-Tabaree, and some are included in this collection of Tafseer, within brackets. Some of the sayings of the scholars about this chain of narration are brought in the next appendix:

APPENDIX THREE:

THE TAFSEER OF `ALEE IBN ABEE TALHAH FROM IBN `ABBAAS -*radiyallaahu `anhumaa.*

*Ibn Abee Haatim said, in 'al-Maraaseel' (p. 118):
"I heard my father say: I heard Duhaym say: "`Alee ibn Abee Talhah did not hear the tafseer from Ibn `Abbaas.'

I heard my father say: I heard Duhaym say: "`Alee ibn Abee Talhah from Ibn `Abbaas is 'mursal' [i.e. has a missing link]. Rather he narrated (it) from Mujaahid, al-Qaasim ibn Muhammad, Raashid ibn Sa`d, and Muhammad ibn Zayd'."

*al-Haafiz Ibn Hajr said, in 'al-`Ujaab fee bayaanil-Asbaab' (p. 58), whilst mentioning the reliable chains of narration for tafseer from Ibn `Abbaas - *radiyallaahu `anhumaa*:
"What is narrated by way of Mu`aawiyah ibn Saalih: from `Alee ibn Abee Talhah: from Ibn `Abbaas.

So `Alee was *sadooq* (truthful/generally acceptable), but he did not meet Ibn `Abbaas. Rather he took it from his reliable students; so therefore al-Bukhaaree, Ibn Abee Haatim, and others relied upon this manuscript."

*Shaikh al-Albaanee said, in 'Jilbaabul-Mar·atil-Muslimah' (p. 88):
"...`Alee, who is Ibn Abee Talhah... Then along with the fact that some of the imaams have spoken about him, then he did not hear from Ibn `Abbaas; nor did he even see him. However it has been said that the link between them is Mujaahid. So if that is correct in this narration, then its chain is fully connected. However the chain of narration to him contains Aboo Saalih, whose name was `Abdullaah ibn Saalih, who had some weakness..."

*as-Suyootee said, in 'al-Itqaan fee `Uloomil-Qur·aan' (2/469-470):
"There is such a large amount of tafseer reported from Ibn `Abbaas that it cannot be enumerated, and there are varying reports and various chains of narrations. So from the good chains of narration is `Alee ibn Abee Talhah al-Haashimee from him."

Ahmad ibn Hanbal said: ‘There is in Egypt a manuscript of tafseer related by `Alee ibn Abee Talhah which is such that if a person were to travel to Egypt just to obtain it, then that would not be too much.’ This is reported with a connected chain of narration by Aboo Ja`far an-Nahhaas in his ‘Naasikh’.

Ibn Hajr said: ‘This manuscript was possessed by Aboo Saalih - the scribe of al-Layth: he narrated it from Mu`aawiyah ibn Saalih: from `Alee ibn Abee Talhah: from Ibn `Abbaas. So al-Bukhaaree possessed it by way of Aboo Saalih, and he depended upon it in his ‘Saheeh’ a great deal in reports from Ibn `Abbaas which he brought without quoting their chain of narration.’

Also Ibn Jareer, Ibn Abee Haatim and Ibn al-Mundhir report plentifully from it, via narrators between themselves and Aboo Saalih.

Some people, though, say: Ibn Abee Talhah did not hear the tafseer from Ibn `Abbaas, but rather he took it from Mujaahid or Sa`eed ibn Jubayr.

Ibn Hajr said: ‘Since the intermediate link is known, and is reliable, there will be no harm in that.’

al-Khaleelee said in ‘al-Irshaad’: ‘The tafseer of Mu`aawiyah ibn Saalih - the Qaadee of al-Andalus-from `Alee ibn Abee Talhah: from Ibn `Abbaas was related by the major narrators from Aboo Saalih - the scribe of al-Layth: from Mu`aawiyah. So the preservers of hadeeth are agreed that Ibn Abee Talhah did not hear [directly] from Ibn `Abbaas.’

With regard to Aboo Saalih the scribe of al-Layth, Ibn Ma`een said: “There are two forms of reliability: reliability of memory and reliability of ones manuscript, and Aboo Saalih - the scribe of al-Layth - was reliable when narrating from his manuscripts.”

Ibn Hajr said of him in ‘Taqreebut-Tahdheeb’: “Sadooq (truthful/acceptable), but he made many mistakes. Reliable when narrating from his manuscripts…..”

APPENDIX FOUR:

BIOGRAPHIES OF THE SALAF WHOSE SAYINGS ARE INCLUDED IN THE TAFSEER.

(Abridged from 'Siyar A`laamin Nubalaa·' of Imaam adh-Dhahabee)

ABOO HURAIRAH -*radiyallaahu `anhu*:

"Aboo Hurairah ad-Dawsee, al-Yamaanee, the great memorizer, the jurist, the Companion of Allaah's Messenger (ﷺ): `Abdur-Rahmaan ibn Sakhr in the most well-known saying.

His name in the times of ignorance was `Abd-Shams. He said: "My father gave me the 'kunyah' of Aboo Hurairah ('Father of the kitten') because I used to tend some sheep and I found some wild kittens. So when he saw them and heard them he said: 'You are the father of the cat,' and my name was `Abd-Shams."

at-Tabaraanee said: His mother -*radiyallaahu `anhaa*- was Maymoonah bint Sabeeh.

Aboo Hurairah performed *hijrah* and arrived at the time of the conquest of Khaybar in the seventh year.

He memorized a huge amount of knowledge from the Prophet (ﷺ), no one else acquired as much as him. He also took from Aboo Bakr, `Umar, Ubayy ibn Ka`b and Ka`b.
Those who narrated from him included al-Agharr Aboo Muslim, Sa`eed ibn al-Musayyib, Basheer ibn Naheek, Hafs ibn `Aasim, Humayd ibn `Abdir-Rahmaan az-Zuhree, Humayd ibn `Abdir-Rahmaan al-Himyaree, Aboo Saalih as-Sammaan, Khallaas ibn `Amr, Saalim Abul-Ghayth, Sa`eed al-Maqburee -and his father Aboo Sa`eed, Sa`eed ibn Marjaanah, Salmaan al-Agharr, Aboo Haazim Salaman al-Ashja`ee, Aboo Yoonus Sulaym ibn Jubayr, Sulaymaan ibn Yasaar, Shahr ibn Hawshab, Saalih mawlaa at-Taw·amah, Damdam ibn Jaus, Taawoos, ash-Sha`bee, Aboo Idrees al-Khawlaanee, Aboo `Uthmaan an-Nahdee, `Abdur-Rahmaan al-A`raj, Iraak

ibn Khaalid, `Ikrimah, `Urwah, `Ataa·, Mujaahid, Ibn Seereen, Muhammad ibn Ziyaad al-Jumahee, Muhammad ibn Ka`b, Moosaa ibn Wardaan, Nu`aym al-Mujmir, Naafi` mawlaa Ibn `Umar, Hammaam ibn Munabbih, and a very great number of people.

He was one of the treasure-houses of knowledge, and one of the major imaams in verdicts, along with his great dignity and excellence, his worship and his humility.

al-Bukhaaree said: Eight hundred people narrated from him."

It is said: He was yellowish-brown, broad-shouldered, having his central incisor teeth widely spaced, he had two locks of hair and he used to dye with red dye. He was a poor man from the people of 'as-Suffah', he experienced hunger and need.

Then after the Prophet (ﷺ) his condition improved and his wealth increased, and he was a person who worshipped and remembered Allaah a great deal. He came to be the governor of al-Madeenah and deputed for Marwaan in his leadership, and he used to pass through the market of al-Madeenah with a bundle of firewood, saying: "Make room on the path for the chief", and he used to joke *-radiyallaahu `anhu.*

Abul-Qaasim ibn Nahhaas: I heard Aboo Bakr ibn Abee Daawood say: "I saw Aboo Hurairah in a dream, whilst I was in Sijjistaan and was compiling his ahaadeeth, and he had a thick beard, was brown, and was wearing coarse clothes. So I said to him: "I love you". So he replied: "I am the first student of ahaadeeth in the world."

Ismaa`eel ibn Abee Khaalid: from Qays: from Aboo Hurairah who said: "When I migrated to the Prophet (ﷺ) I said along the way: 'Oh what a long wearing night; yet it brought about rescue from the land of Unbelief'." He said: "And a slave belonging to me ran away. So when I came and gave the pledge of allegiance the slave appeared, so the Prophet (ﷺ) said: << This is your slave, O Hurairah. >> So I said: "He is free for the Face of Allaah", so I set him free."
[al-Bukhaaree: (no. 2531)]

-Ayyoob: from Muhammad: that Aboo Hurairah used to say to his daughter: "Do not wear gold, because I fear for you the blazing flame."

-Saalim ibn Hayyaan: from his father: from Aboo Hurairah that he said: I grew up as an orphan, and performed Hijrah as a poor man, and I used to be a hired worker for the daughter of Ghazwaan and my wages were food for my stomach and a turn upon the riding beast. So I would drive the camels along when they rode, and I would collect firewood when they stopped somewhere. So All praise is for Allaah Who gave strength and authority to the Religion and Who made Aboo Hurairah an Imaam."

-az-Zuhree: from Saalim: that he heard Aboo Hurairah say: "A people in the state of *ihraam* asked me about people not in the state of *ihraam* giving them as a gift some game that had been hunted, so I told them to eat it. Then I met `Umar and informed him of this, so he said: 'If you had given them a different verdict I would have punished you'."

-Qays ibn Abee Haazim: from Aboo Hurairah who said: "I came on the day of Khaybar after they had finished fighting."

-Ibn Seereen said: Aboo Hurairah said: "I would sometimes faint between the grave and the minbar because of severe hunger to the extent that the people would say: 'He is possessed', so a man would sit upon my chest. So I would raise up my head and say: "It is not what you think, it is just hunger."

-Ahmad narrated in his 'Musnad' from Aboo Katheer as-Suhaymee from Aboo Hurairah who said: Allaah's Messenger (ﷺ) said: << O Allaah make this slave of yours -meaning Aboo Hurairah- and his mother beloved to your believing servants, and make them beloved to the two of them. >>
[Muslim: (2491)]

-Ibn Abee Dhi·b: from al-Maqburee: from Aboo Hurairah who said: " I preserved two sack-fulls of knowledge from Allaah's Messenger (ﷺ). So as for one of them, then I distributed it amongst the people; and as for the other one, then if I had opened it, then my throat would have been cut off." [[al-Bukhaaree: (no. 120): Ibn Hajr said in 'Fathul-Baaree': The scholars understand the sack of knowledge which he did not spread to be the ahaadeeth which gave the names of the evil rulers, and their conditions, and

their times; and Aboo Hurairah used to allude to some of that but not state it plainly, out of fear of them for himself.]]
-al-A`mash: from Aboo Saalih as-Sammaan who said: "Aboo Hurairah was one of the greatest memorizers amongst the Companions of Allaah's Messenger (ﷺ)."

-ash-Shaafi`ee said: "Aboo Hurairah was the greatest memorizer who narrated hadeeth in his time."

Kahmas narrated from `Abdullaah ibn Shaqeeq who said: Aboo Hurairah said: "I do not know anyone from the Companions of Allaah's Messenger (ﷺ) who memorized more of his ahaadeeth than me."

-Aboo Daawood at-Tayaalisee: `Imraan al-Qattaan related to us: from Bakr ibn `Abdillaah: from Aboo Raafi`: from Aboo Hurairah that he met Ka`b and began narrating to him and asking him. So Ka`b said: "I have not seen anyone who has not read the Tawraat having better knowledge of what is contained in it than Aboo Hurairah."

-Hushaym: from Ya`laa ibn `Ataa·: from al-Waleed ibn `Abdir-Rahmaan: from Ibn `Umar that he said: "O Aboo Hurairah: You were the one amongst us who most closely accompanied Allaah's Messenger (ﷺ) and the most knowledgeable of us of his ahaadeeth."

-Hammaad ibn Zayd: from `Abbaas al-Jurayree: I heard Aboo `Uthmaan an-Nahdee who said: "I took Aboo Hurairah as a guest for seven days; so he, his wife and his servant followed each other, dividing the night into three. One would pray and then awaken the next who would pray, and would then awaken the third."

-Ibraaheem ibn Yoosuf related to us: Ibn Rawaahah related to us: as-Silafee related to us: Ibn al-Busree related to us: as-Sukkaree related to us: as-Saffaar related to us: ar-Ramaadee related to us: `Abdur-Razzaaq related to us: Ma`mar related to us: from Muhammad ibn Ziyaad who said: "Mu`aawiyah used to appoint Aboo Hurairah to be the governor of al-Madeenah, but if he became angry with him he would send Marwaan to replace him, but it would not be long before he would re-appoint Aboo Hurairah and remove Marwaan. So he said to a black slave: "Stand at the door and do not prevent anyone from entering except Marwaan. So the servant did so. Then later when it became the turn of Marwaan he entered and said: "We were prevented (from entry)!" So he replied: "The one having the most right that I should not deny him is you."

Khuthaym ibn `Iraak narrated from his father: from Aboo Hurairah that he said: "The Prophet (ﷺ) had gone off to Khaybar when I came as a muhaajir to al-Madeenah. So I prayed the Dawn Prayer behind Sibaa` ibn `Urfutah- whom he had left in charge and in the first rak`ah he recited Soorah Maryam, and in the other one

﴿وَيْلٌ لِّلْمُطَفِّفِينَ﴾

[*Sooratul-Mutaffifeen*]

So I said: "Woe to my father! How rare it is to find a man in the land of the Azd except that he has two measures: a measure for himself and another one to short-change the people with."

Humayd ibn `Abdir-Rahmaan al-Himyaree said: "He accompanied (the Prophet (ﷺ) for four years."

He suffered hunger and poverty, and adhered to the mosque. When he migrated he had a slave of his along with him but he fled and got away.

Hishaam: from Muhammad [i.e. Ibn Seereen] who said: we were in the presence of Aboo Hurairah [and he was wearing two linen garments dyed with red clay], and he blew his nose and wiped it upon his upper garment and said: "All praise is for Allaah who has provided Aboo Hurairah with linen to blow his nose on! For I have seen a time when I would faint between the house of `Aa·ishah and the minbar because of severe hunger. So then a man would pass by and sit upon my chest [thinking that I had become possessed]. So I would raise up my head and say: "It is not what you think, it is just hunger."
[[al-Bukhaaree: no. 7324]]

I [i.e. adh-Dhahabee] say: Those who saw him would think that he was possessed, and so sit on him to recite 'ruqyah' upon him, or the like.

...from `Aamir: from Aboo Hurairah that he said: "I was in as-Suffah [[a shaded place at the rear of the mosque of the Prophet (ﷺ) where the poor and those with no accommodation would stay]] so Allaah's Messenger (ﷺ) sent some `Ajwah dates to us, so we would take two dates together because of our hunger; and when one of us wanted to take two dates at a time he would say to his companion: I am taking two dates at a time, so do likewise."
[['as-Saheehah': 2323]]

Mujaahid narrated: that Aboo Hurairah used to say: "By Allaah, besides Whom none has the right to be worshipped, I used to lay down on the ground resting upon my liver because of hunger, and I used to tie a stone upon my belly because of hunger. One day I sat by the way where the people would come out, and Aboo Bakr passed by. So I asked him about an Aayah from the Book of Allaah, and I only asked him so that he would satisfy my hunger, but then he carried on and did not do so. Then `Umar passed by me and so I asked him about an Aayah from the Book of Allaah, and I only asked him so that he would satisfy my hunger, but then he carried on and did not do so. Then Abul-Qaasim (ﷺ) passed by me and smiled when he saw me and recognized what was in my heart and on my face. He said: << O Aboo Hirr! >> I replied: "At your service, O Messenger of Allaah." He said: << Follow me >>. So he proceeded and I followed him, and he entered his house. So I requested permission to enter and was admitted. So he entered and found some milk in a bowl. So he said: << Where is this milk from? >> So they said: 'It was presented as a gift by such and such man, or such and such woman.' He said: << O Aboo Hirr! >> I said: "At your service, O Messenger of Allaah!" He said: << go to the people of 'Suffah' and call them to me >> and the people of 'Suffah' were the guests of Islaam: they did not have families, wealth or any person to support them. So whenever some charity came to him he would send it to them, and he would not take anything from it himself; and whenever something was sent to him as a gift he would send something to them and take some of it himself, and cause them to share in it. So his order upset me and I said (to myself): 'How will this small quantity of milk be enough for the people of 'as-Suffah'?!' I felt I was more entitled to drink from that milk in order to strengthen myself by it. But if they came, then he would command me to give it to them; and then what would remain of that milk for me?!' However I could not but obey Allaah and obey His Messenger (ﷺ). So I went to them and invited them and they came. So they sought permission to enter and he admitted

them. So they took their seats in the house. He said: << O Aboo Hirr! >> I said "At your service, O Messenger of Allaah!" He said: << Take it and give it to them. >> So I took it and started by giving it to one man who drank until he was full, and then he returned it to me. Then I gave it to the next man who drank until he was full and then returned it to me, until I came to the Prophet (ﷺ) and all of the people had drank until they were full. So he took the bowl and placed it upon his hand, then he looked at me and smiled, and said: << O Aboo Hirr! >> I said: "At your service, O Messenger of Allaah!" He said: << There remain I and you. >> I said: "You have spoken the truth, O Messenger of Allaah." He said: << Sit down and drink. >> So I sat down and drank. He said: << Drink! >> So I drank, and he kept on saying: "Drink!" until I said: "No, by the One Who sent you with the truth, I have no more room for it." He said: << Hand it to me. >> So I gave him the bowl, and he praised Allaah and mentioned Allaah's Name upon it and drank the remainder."
[al-Bukhaaree: (no. 6452)]

...Aboo Katheer as-Suhaymee and his name was Yazeed ibn `Abdir-Rahmaan narrated: that Aboo Hurairah narrated to me, saying: "By Allaah, Allaah has not created a true Believer who hears of me except that he loves me." I said: 'How do you know that?' He said: "My mother was a Mushrik woman, and I used to call her to Islaam but she would not accept it from me. So I called her one day but she said something disagreeable to me about Allaah's Messenger (ﷺ). So I went to Allaah's Messenger (ﷺ) and I was weeping. So I informed him and asked him to supplicate for her, so he said: << O Allaah guide the mother of Aboo Hurairah. >> So then I went out running to give her the good news. So I arrived and the door was closed and I heard the splashing of water, and she heard the sound of my footsteps. So she said: 'Wait as you are!' Then she opened the door, and she had put her gown on, and had been too hasty to put on her khimaar. So she said: 'I testify that none has the right to be worshipped except Allaah, and that Muhammad is His Slave and His Messenger.' He said: "So I went back to Allaah's Messenger (ﷺ) weeping with joy just as I had wept from sorrow, and I informed him, and I said: "Make supplication to Allaah that he should cause me and my mother to be beloved to His believing servants. So he said: << O Allaah make this slave of Yours and his mother beloved to Your believing servants, and cause them to be loved by these two. >>" -"Its chain of narration is 'hasan'."

[[Reported by Ahmad (2/319-320), and Muslim (no. 2491)]]

Ibn Shihaab: from Sa`eed [Ibn al-Musayyib] and Aboo Salamah: that Aboo Hurairah said: "You people say that 'Aboo Hurairah narrates too many ahaadeeth from Allaah's Messenger (ﷺ)! And you say that why is it not the case that the Muhaajiroon and the Ansaar do not narrate like him!' But my brothers from the Muhaajiroon were busy in the markets, and my brothers from the Ansaar were busy working upon their property. But I was a poor man from the poor people of 'as-Suffah'. I used to adhere to Allaah's Messenger (ﷺ) and be content with what filled my stomach. So I would be present when they were absent, and remember when they would forget; and Allaah's Messenger (ﷺ) said to us one day:
<< No one will spread out his garment till I have finished what I am saying, and then gather his garment upon himself except that he will preserve whatever I say. >>
So I spread out a striped cloak which I had upon me until he finished what he was saying, and then gathered it upon my chest. So I did not forget anything from that narration."
[[al-Bukhaaree (no. 2047) and Muslim (no. 2492)]]

az-Zuhree, also: from al-A`raj: from Aboo Hurairah who said: "You claim that I narrate excessively from Allaah's Messenger (ﷺ)! Whereas the truth is known by Allaah. I was a poor man who accompanied Allaah's Messenger (ﷺ) and contented myself with whatever filled my stomach. So he narrated to us one day and said:
<< Whoever will spread out his garment, will never forget anything which he heard from me. >> So I did so, and by the One Who sent him with the truth I have never forgotten anything which I heard from him."
[[al-Bukhaaree (nos. 118 & 2350); Muslim (no. 2492)]]

...al-Maqburee: from Aboo Hurairah who said: I said: "O Messenger of Allaah who will be the most fortunate of people to attain your intercession?" He said: << I thought that none would ask me about this before you, because I have seen your eagerness upon learning hadeeth: The most fortunate of the people to attain my intercession on the day of resurrection will be whoever says: 'None has the right to be worshipped except Allaah', sincerely from his heart. >>
[[al-Bukhaaree (no. 99)]]

ash-Shaafi`ee said: "Aboo Hurairah was the best memorizer of those who narrated hadeeth in his time."

...from Hammaam [ibn Munabbih] who said: I heard Aboo Hurairah say: "There is no one from the Companions of Allaah's Messenger (ﷺ) who has more hadeeth than me, except for `Abdullaah ibn `Amr because he used to write, whereas I did not write."
[[al-Bukhaaree (no. 113)]]

`Abdul-Waahid ibn Ziyaad and others: `Aasim ibn Kulayb narrated to us: My father narrated to us that he heard Aboo Hurairah, and he used to begin narrating hadeeth by saying: "Allaah's Messenger (ﷺ) said: << Who ever lies upon me deliberately, then let him take his place in the Fire. >>"
[[Ahmad: (2/413)]]

...from Ibn `Umar that he said to Aboo Hurairah: "O Aboo Hurairah! You were the one from us who most closely adhered to Allaah's Messenger (ﷺ), and the one from us who best memorized his ahaadeeth."
[['Saheeh Sunanit-Tirmidhee (no. 3836)]]

Aboo Hurairah passed away in the year 58 H, and this was stated by a group; and others said: 59 H; and it was said: 57 H *-radiyallaahu `anhu-* at the age of 78."

`ABDULLAAH IBN `ABBAAS *-radiyallaahu `anhumaa*:

"`Abdullaah ibn `Abbaas ibn `Abdul-Muttalib *-radiyallaahu `anhumaa-* the Imaam, the ocean of knowledge, the great scholar (habr) of the Ummah, and the Imaam of Tafseer.

Abul-`Abbaas, al-Haashimee, the son of the paternal uncle of Allaah's Messenger (ﷺ), and the father of the khulafaa· [i.e. the later `Abbaasid caliphs.]

He was born in the mountain pass of Banoo Haashim, three years before the Hijrah. He accompanied the Prophet (ﷺ) for about thirty months, and

Allaah's Messenger (ﷺ) died when he was thirteen years old. The Prophet (ﷺ) supplicated for him that Allaah should grant him knowledge and understanding of the Religion, and should teach him explanation of the Book.

Khaalid al-Hadhdhaa· said: from `Ikrimah: from Ibn `Abbaas who said: The Prophet (ﷺ) stroked my head and supplicated for wisdom for me."

-Aboo `Aasim: Shabeeb ibn Bishr related to us: `Ikrimah related to us: from Ibn `Abbaas who said: "Allaah's Messenger (ﷺ) went to relieve himself, then he moved away and found a covered pot (of water), so he said: << Who brought this? >> So `Abdullaah (ibn `Abbaas) said: "It was I", so he said: << O Allaah teach him explanation of the Qur·aan. >>
[Saheeh: 'Sharhut-Tahaawiyyah' (no. 180), 'as-Saheehah' (no. 2589)]

-al-A`mash: from `Abud-Duhaa: from Masrooq who said: Ibn Mas`ood said: "What a fine explainer of the Qur·aan is Ibn `Abbaas! If he had reached our age, then none of us would have attained a tenth of his knowledge."

-al-A`mash: from Aboo Waa·il: "`Alee placed Ibn `Abbaas in charge of the Hajj, so he gave a khutbah that day which was such that if it had been heard by the Turks and the Romans they would have accepted Islaam. Then he recited Sooratun-Noor to them and began explaining it."

He narrated a good number of narrations from the Prophet (ﷺ), and from `Umar. `Alee, Mu`aadh, his father al-`Abbaas, `Abdur-Rahmaan ibn `Awf, Aboo Sufyaan Sakhr ibn Harb, Aboo Dharr, Ubayy ibn Ka`b, Zayd ibn Thaabit, and a large number of others.

He recited Qur·aan with Ubayy (ibn Ka`b) and Zayd (ibn Thaabit).
Mujaahid, Sa`eed ibn Jubayr, and a group took the recitation from him. Those who narrated from him are: his son `Alee, the son of his brother `Abdullaah ibn Ma`bad, and his freed slaves: `Ikrimah, Miqsam, and Aboo Ma`bad Naafidh; and Anas ibn Maalik, Abut-Tufayl, Aboo Umaamah ibn Sahl, and his brother Katheer ibn `Abbaas; and `Urwah ibn az-Zubayr, `Ubaydullaah ibn `Umar, Taawoos, Abush-Sha`thaa· Jaabir, `Alee ibn al-Husayn, Sa`eed ibn Jubayr, Mujaahid ibn Jabr, al-Qaasim ibn Muhammad, Aboo Saalih as-Sammaan, Aboo Rajaa· al-`Utaaridee, Abul-`Aaliyah,

`Ubayd ibn `Umayr and his son `Abdullaah `Ataa· ibn Yasaar, Ibraaheem ibn `Abdullaah ibn Ma`bad, and Arbadah at-Tameemee - the companion of the 'Tafseer', and Aboo Saalih Baadhaam, Taleeq ibn Qays al-Hanafee, `Ataa· ibn Abee Rabaah, ash-Sha`bee, al-Hasan, Ibn Seereen, Muhammad ibn Ka`b al-Qurazee, Shahr ibn Hawshab, Ibn Mulaykah, `Amr ibn Deenaar, `Ubaydullaah ibn Abee Yazeed, Aboo Jamrah Nasr ibn `Imraan ad-Duba`ee ad-Dahhaak ibn Muzaahim, Abuz-Zubayr al-Makkee, Bakr ibn `Abdullaah al-Muzanee, Habeeb ibn Abee Thaabit, Sa`eed ibn Abil-Hasan, Ismaa`eel as-Suddee, and many others besides them.

And 'at-Tahdheeb' mentions a hundred and ninety seven people who narrated from him.

-al-Madaa·inee: from Nu`aym ibn Hafs: that Aboo Bakr said: "Ibn `Abbaas came to us in Basrah, and there was not anyone the like of him amongst the `Arabs in his body, his knowledge, his explanation , his handsomeness and his completeness."

-`Abdur-Razzaaq: from Ma`mar who said: "The greater part of the knowledge of Ibn `Abbaas was taken from three men: `Umar, `Alee and Ubayy ibn Ka`b *-radiyallaahu `anhum.*

-Aboo Bakr ibn `Ayyaash: from Muhammad ibn `Amr: from Aboo Salamah: from Ibn `Abbaas who said: "I used to hear that a man would have a hadeeth, so I would go to him and sit until he came out. So then I would ask him; and if I had wished I could have got him to come out to me."

-Zaa·idah: `Abdur-Rahmaan ibn `Abdullaah ibn al-Asbahaanee related to us: that `Abdullaah ibn Shaddaad, will you not be amazed? A boy came to me after I had laid down to take the noon siesta, and said: 'There is a man at the door requesting permission to enter.' So I said: "He must have come for some need, so grant him permission to enter." He said: So he entered and said: 'Will you not inform me about that man.' So I said: "Which man?" So he said: "`Alee ibn Abee Taalib: when will he be returned to life?' So I said: "Subhaan Allaah! (I declare Allaah free of all imperfections!) When everybody in the graves is resurrected." So he said: 'I do not see except that you are saying the same as those stupid people.' So I said: "Get him out or I will beat him."

-Ma`mar: from Qataadah: from Mutarrif who said: "I heard Ibn `Abbaas say: "Revising knowledge for an hour is better than spending the whole night awake (in Prayer)."
His mother was Ummul-Fadl Lubaabah bint al-Haarith ibn Huzn ibn Bujayr al-Hilaaliyyah, descended from Hilaal ibn `Aamir.

He had a group of children; the eldest being al `Abbaas -after whom he took his kunyah; and `Alee -the father of the khulafaa· and he was the youngest of them, and al-Fadl, and Muhammad, and `Ubaydullaah, and Lubaabah and Asmaa·.

He was a person who was pleasant-looking and handsome, tall in stature, imposing, complete intellect, quick in understanding, a man complete in his characteristics.

His children al-Fadl, Muhammad and `Ubaydullaah died without offspring; whereas Lubaabah produced children and descendants from her husband `Alee ibn `Abdullaah ibn Ja`far ibn Abee Taalib; and his other daughter Asmaa·, who was married to her paternal cousin `Abdullaah ibn `Ubaydullaah ibn al-`Abbaas, gave birth to Hasan and Husayn.

Ibn `Abbaas went with his parents to the place of Hijrah [al-Madeenah] in the year of the Conquest, having accepted Islaam before that. So it is established from him that he said: "I and my mother were from the weak ones (who were excused from migrating): I was a child and my mother from the women."

Khaalid al-Hadhdhaa·: from `Ikrimah: from Ibn `Abbaas that he said: "The Prophet (ﷺ) wiped my head and supplicated for wisdom for me. [[al-Bukhaaree's narration (no. 75) is: "Once the Prophet (ﷺ) embraced me and said: << O Allaah bestow upon him knowledge of the Book >>.]]

Ibn Shihaab narrated: from `Ubaydullaah: from Ibn `Abbaas who said: "I came riding an ass, and I was close to puberty, and Allaah's Messenger (ﷺ) was leading the people in Prayer in Minaa."
[[al-Bukhaaree: no. 492]...

Aboo Sa`eed ibn Yoonus said: Ibn `Abbaas went on military expedition to Africa with Ibn Abee Sarh; and fifteen of the people of Egypt narrated from him."

Aboo `Abdillaah ibn Mandah said: "His mother was Ummul-Fadl, the sister of Ummul-Mu·mineen Maymoonah, and he was born two years before the Hijrah."

He was light-skinned and tall; his complexion was tinged with yellow. He was stout and he was handsome, fair of face, and he had hair up to the ears. He dyed with henna, and the Prophet (ﷺ) supplicated for wisdom for him.
I say: He was the maternal cousin of Khaalid ibn al-Waleed al-Makhzoomee.

Sa`eed ibn Saalim narrated: Ibn Jurayj narrated to us, saying: we were sitting with `Ataa· in al-Masjidul-Haraam and were speaking about Ibn `Abbaas. So `Ataa· said: "I never see the moon on the fourteenth night [[i.e. when full and bright]] except that it reminds me of the face of Ibn `Abbaas."

Ibraaheem ibn al-Hakam ibn Abaan narrated: from his father: from `Ikrimah who said: "When Ibn `Abbaas passed along a path-way the women in the walled gardens would say: 'Is it musk that has gone by, or was it Ibn `Abbaas?'."...

Hammaad ibn Salamah and others narrate: from `Abdullaah ibn `Uthmaan ibn Khuthaym: from Sa`eed ibn Jubayr: from `Abdullaah [Ibn `Abbaas who said: "I spent the night in the house of my maternal aunt Maymoonah and I placed some water for the Prophet (ﷺ) to take a bath, so he said: << Who has placed this? >> So they said: '`Abdullaah', so he said: << O Allaah grant him knowledge of explanation, and grant him understanding of the Religion. >> [[Saheeh: Ahmad, at-Tabaraanee...]]

Aboo Zur`ah ad-Dimashqee reports in his 'Taareekh' from Ibn `Umar that he said: "He [i.e. Ibn `Abbaas] is the most knowledgeable of the people regarding that which Allaah sent down to Muhammad."

Aboo Nu`aym reports in 'al-Hilyah' from Shaqeeq who said: "Ibn `Abbaas delivered a khutbah to us whilst he was in charge of the Hajj. So he started reciting Sooratul-Baqarah. So he would recite and then explain. So I began saying to myself: I have never seen or heard the speech of a man the like of it; if the Persians and the Romans were to hear it they would enter into Islaam. ....

Saalih ibn Rustum al-Khazzaaz narrated: from Ibn Abee Mulaykah: I accompanied Ibn `Abbaas from Makkah to al-Madeenah. So when he camped at a place he would spend half of the night standing in Prayer. So Ayyoob asked him: 'How had his recitation used to be?' He said: He recited:

﴿ وَجَآءَتْ سَكْرَةُ ٱلْمَوْتِ بِٱلْحَقِّ ذَٰلِكَ مَا كُنتَ مِنْهُ تَحِيدُ ﴾

[*Soorah Qaaf (50): 19*]

[[Meaning: And the stupor of death will come in truth: this is what you sought to flee from]]. So he would recite it slowly and carefully, and be sobbing a great deal."

Ibn Jurayj narrated: from Ibn Abee Mulaykah: that Ibn `Abbaas said: "The people have passed away and the apes remain." It was said: 'What are the 'apes'?' So he replied: "Those who resemble the people but are not people."

Ibn Taawoos narrated: from his father: from Ibn `Abbaas: "Mu`aawiyah said to me: 'Are you upon the way of `Alee?!' So I replied: 'No, nor upon the way of `Uthmaan. I am upon the way of Allaah's Messenger (ﷺ)."

From Taawoos who said: "I did not see anyone greater in the respect they showed to Allaah's prohibitions than Ibn `Abbaas [and whenever I remember him I wished I would weep].

Jareer ibn Haazim narrated: from Ya`laa ibn Hakeem: from `Ikrimah: from Ibn `Abbaas who said: "When Allaah's Messenger (ﷺ) passed away, I said to a man from the Ansaar: "Come let us ask questions of the Companions of Allaah's Messenger (ﷺ) because they are many at this time." So he said: 'How surprising of you, O Ibn `Abbaas! Do you think that the people will come to need you, when there are amongst the people the Companions of the Prophet (ﷺ) those whom you see?!' So he left that ,and I began asking. So whenever I heard that a man had a hadeeth I would go to him whilst he was taking the noon siesta. So I would place my cloak as a pillow at his door, and the wind would blow dust over me. Then the man would come out and see me and say: "O cousin of Allaah's Messenger! Why didn't you send a message so that I should come to you?' So I would say: "It is more fitting that I should come to you and ask you." So the man [of the Ansaar] remained until he found the people gathering around me, so he said 'This youth was more intelligent than me.'"

`Abdul-Malik ibn Abee Sulaymaan narrated from Sa`eed ibn Jubayr who said: "Some men of the Muhaajiroon felt that they had a grievance with `Umar because of the fact that he brought Ibn `Abbaas close to him [in gatherings] and did not do so with them; and he used to question him. So `Umar said: "Today I will show you something that will cause you to recognize his excellence." So he asked them about this Soorah:

﴿إِذَا جَآءَ نَصۡرُ ٱللَّهِ وَٱلۡفَتۡحُ﴾

[*Sooratun-Nasr (110)*]

So some of them said: 'It is a command from Allaah for His Prophet that when he saw them entering into Allaah's Religion in crowds he was to praise Him and seek His forgiveness.' So `Umar said: 'O Ibn `Abbaas! Speak!' So he said: "He informed him when he was going to die. Meaning: It will be a sign for the approach of your death, so praise your Lord and seek His forgiveness." [[So `Umar said: I do not know about it except what you have said.]]

Yazeed ibn Ibraaheem narrated: from Sulaymaan al-Ahwal: from Taawoos: from Ibn `Abbaas that he said: "Concerning a single matter I would ask thirty of the Companions of the Prophet (ﷺ)." Its chain of narration is 'Saheeh'…

From `Ikrimah: I heard Mu`aawiyah say to me: "Your master [i.e. Ibn `Abbaas], by Allaah, is the most knowledgeable one of those who have died and those who are alive."

And it is related from `Aa·ishah that she said: "The most knowledgeable person about the Hajj who remains is Ibn `Abbaas."
I say: And he used to hold Hajj Tamattu` as being what is essential.

..Ibn Jurayj narrated: from Taawoos who said: I did not see anyone with more piety than Ibn `Umar, nor anyone more knowledgeable than Ibn `Abbaas."

Mujaahid said: "I never saw anyone the like of Ibn `Abbaas; and he was, at the time he died, the great scholar of this Ummaah."

al-A`mash narrated: from Mujaahid who said: "Ibn `Abbaas used to be called 'the ocean' (al-Bahr) because of his extensive knowledge."...

Masrooq narrated, saying: "When I would see Ibn `Abbaas I would say: 'He is the most handsome of the people', and when he uttered something I would say: 'He is the most eloquent of the people', and when he talked I would say: 'He is the most knowledgeable of the people.'

al-Qaasim ibn Muhammad said: "I never saw anything futile in the gathering of Ibn `Abbaas."...

Aboo `Awaanah narrated: from Abul-Juwayriyah who said: 'I saw the Izaar of Ibn `Abbaas half way down his shins, or above that and he had a roman cloak upon him and he was praying.'...

Ibn Hazm said in his book 'al-Ihkaam': Aboo Bakr Muhammad ibn Moosaa ibn Ya`qoob ibn al-Ma·moon, one of the imaams of Islaam, gathered together the verdicts of Ibn `Abbaas in twenty volumes.

The debate of Ibn `Abbaas *-radiyallaahu `anhumaa-* with the Khawaarijee which resulted in the majority of them returning from their innovation to the truth:

AT-TABARAANEE reported in 'al-Mu`jamul Kabeer' (no. 10598): "Ishaaq ibn Ibraaheem ad-Dabaree narrated to us: from `Abdur-Razzaaq. Further Isnaad: And `Alee ibn `Abdil-`Azeez narrated to us: Aboo Hudhayfah Moosaa ibn Mas`ood narrated to us: both of them from `Ikrimah ibn `Ammaar that Aboo Zameel al-Hanafee narrated to us: that `Abdullaah ibn `Abbaas narrated to us, saying:
"When the (Khawaarij) separated themselves off in Haarooraa and gathered themselves together in some abode. So I said to `Alee: "O Ameerul-

Mu·mineen pray the Prayer in its earliest time so that I can then go and speak to those people." So he said: 'I fear for you from them.' So I dressed in the best clothes I could and wore this Yemeni cloak. So I went to them and entered upon them whilst they were resting at the time of the start of the afternoon heat. So I entered upon a people who were such that I have never seen a people who strove harder in worship than them. Their hands were like the knees of camels, and their faces were scarred with the traces of prostration. So when I entered they said: 'Welcome, O Ibn `Abbaas, what has brought you here?' So he said: "I came to narrate to you from the Companions of Allaah's Messenger (ﷺ): the Revelation came down and they know best about its explanation." So some of them said: 'Don't speak with him' and others said: 'Rather we will speak with him.' He said: I said: "Tell me the criticism you have of the son of the uncle of Allaah's Messenger (ﷺ), his son in law, and the first of those who believed in him; and the Companions of Allaah's Messenger (ﷺ) are along with him." They said: 'We criticize him for three things.' I said: "What are they?" They said: 'The first of them is that he caused men to pass judgement in Allaah's Religion, whereas Allaah said: ﴿إِنِ ٱلْحُكْمُ إِلَّا لِلَّهِ﴾ [*Soorah Yoosuf (12): 40*]

[[Meaning: Judgement is only for Allaah]].' He said: "And what else?"
So they said: 'He fought but did not take any females captured as slaves-girls, nor did he seize war-booty. So if the enemy were Disbelievers, then their property was lawful for us; and if they were Believers, then it was forbidden for us to shed their blood.' He said: I said: "And what else?" They said: 'He erased his title 'Ameerul-Mu·mineen' (chief of the Believers), so if he is not the chief of the Believers, then he must be the chief of the Disbelievers.' He said: I said: "What do you think if I recite to you from the decisive Book of Allaah, and I narrate to you from the Sunnah of your Prophet (ﷺ) that which you cannot deny, will you turn back?" They said: 'Yes'. He said: So I said: "As for your saying that he caused men to judge in Allaah's Religion, then He says:

﴿يَٰٓأَيُّهَا ٱلَّذِينَ ءَامَنُوا۟ لَا تَقْتُلُوا۟ ٱلصَّيْدَ وَأَنتُمْ حُرُمٌ﴾ up to His Saying:

﴿يَحْكُمُ بِهِۦ ذَوَا عَدْلٍ مِّنكُمْ﴾ [*Sooratul-Maa·idah (5): Aayah 95*]

[[Meaning: O you who believe, do not kill game whilst in a state of *i<u>h</u>raam*; and whoever of you does that intentionally, then the penalty is a sacrifice equal to the animal killed, as adjudged by two just men among you.]]

And said, with regard to a woman and her husband:

﴿ وَإِنْ خِفْتُمْ شِقَاقَ بَيْنِهِمَا فَٱبْعَثُوا۟ حَكَمًا مِّنْ أَهْلِهِۦ وَحَكَمًا مِّنْ أَهْلِهَآ ﴾

[*Sooratun-Nisaa· (4): 35*]

[[Meaning: If you fear a breach between the husband and wife then send an arbitrator from his family and an arbitrator from her family]]

I adjure you by Allaah; does the judgement of men for the sparing of their blood and their persons and rectification of relations between them have more right, or their judgement with regard to a rabbit whose price is a quarter of a dirham?" They said: 'O Allaah: For sparing their blood and rectifying between them.' He said: "Have you abandoned this criticism?" They said: 'O Allaah, yes.'

Then as for your saying that they fought but did not take captured females as slave-girls and did not take war-booty: then would you take your mother as a slave-girl and make lawful from her that which you make lawful regarding other then her, for in that case you would be Disbelievers; and if you claim that she [i.e. `Aa·ishah-*radiyallaahu `anhaa*] is not your mother, then you are Disbelievers and have left Islaam because Allaah -the Mighty and Majestic-says:

﴿ ٱلنَّبِىُّ أَوْلَىٰ بِٱلْمُؤْمِنِينَ مِنْ أَنفُسِهِمْ ۖ وَأَزْوَٰجُهُۥٓ أُمَّهَـٰتُهُمْ ﴾

[*Sooratul-Ahzaab (33): 6*]

[[Meaning: The Prophet has more right upon the Believers than their own selves, and his wives are as their mothers]]:
so you are between two deviations and may choose whichever of them you please. Do you abandon this argument?" They said: 'O Allaah, yes.'
He said: "As for your saying that he erased his title of 'Ameerul-Mu·mineen', then Allaah's Messenger (ﷺ) called, on the day of Hudaybiyyah to write an agreement between him and them. So he said: << Write: This is the judgement agreed to by Muhammad, the Messenger of Allaah. >> So they said: 'By Allaah, if we knew you to be Allaah's Messenger we would not prevent you from the House, nor would we have fought against you. But rather write: Muhammad the son of `Abdullaah.' So

he said: << By Allaah I am the Messenger of Allaah even if you reject me. Write, O `Alee: Muhammad the son of `Abdullaah. >>
So Allaah's Messenger (ﷺ) was more excellent than `Alee. So do you abandon this criticism?" They said: 'O Allaah, yes.'
So twenty thousand of them returned and four thousand remained and were killed."
[Hasan: 'as-Saheehul-Musnad min Fadaa·ilis-Sahaabah' of Mustafaa al-`Adawee (pp. 427-428)].

Ibn `Abbaas died in Taa·if in the year 68 H, and Muhammad ibn al-Hanafiyyah [the son of `Alee ibn Abee Taalib and Khawlah bint al-Hanafiyyah] lead the funeral prayer over him, and said: "Today the wise scholar (*rabbaanee*) of this Ummah has died." -*radiyallaahu `anhumaa.*

`ABDULLAAH IBN `AMR -*radiyallaahu `anhumaa*:

`Abdullaah ibn `Amr ibn al-`Aas ibn Waa·il ibn Haashim ibn Sa`eed ibn Sa`d ibn Sahm ibn `Amr ibn Husays ibn Ka`b ibn Lu·ayy ibn Ghaalib, the Imaam, the great scholar, the worshipper. The Companion of Allaah's Messenger (ﷺ) and the son of his Companion.

Aboo Muhammad and it is said: Aboo `Abdir-Rahmaan, and it is said: Aboo Naseer; al-Qurashee, as-Sahmee.

His mother was Raa·itah bint al-Hajjaaj ibn Munabbih as-Sahmiyyah.

His father was no older than him except by eleven years or thereabouts.

It has reached us that he accepted Islaam before his father; and it is said that his name was 'al-`Aas' [the disobedient one], so when he accepted Islaam the Prophet (ﷺ) changed it to `Abdullaah.

He possessed many merits and virtues, and had a high position with regard to knowledge and action. He carried a great deal of knowledge from the Prophet (ﷺ).

He was one of those who performed the Hijrah along with his father prior to the conquest of Makkah. His father was only eleven years older than him. The Prophet (ﷺ) used to prefer him over his father, and in the time of the Prophet (ﷺ) he was a person who fasted a great deal, stood in (Night) Prayer a great deal, and recited the Qur·aan a great deal, and who sought a great deal of knowledge.

He wrote down a lot of knowledge from the Prophet (ﷺ), and Aboo Hurairah acknowledged the great amount of knowledge he possessed, and said: “Because he used to write things down from the Prophet (ﷺ) and I had not used to write.”

The ahaadeeth he narrates from the Prophet (ﷺ) reach seven hundred in number. al-Bukhaaree and Muslim were united in reporting seven of his ahaadeeth, al-Bukhaaree was alone in reporting eight, and Muslim twenty.

He wrote down a great deal of narrations with the permission of the Prophet (ﷺ)…

`Abdullaah also narrated from Aboo Bakr, `Umar, Mu`aadh, Suraaqah ibn Maalik, and his father `Amr, and `Abdur-Rahmaan ibn `Awf, Abud-Dardaa· and a group; also from the people of the Book, and he closely examined their books and gave attention to that.

He was a person of excellence and was earnest in his affairs, and he criticized his father for taking part in affairs in the time of tribulation; however he feared falling into the sin of disobedience if he abandoned his father, so he was therefore present at the battle of Siffeen, but he did not unsheathe a sword.

He acquired a number of the books of the People of the Book and closely examined them, and found some amazing things in them.

His father left him a vast amount of property, and he possessed slaves and servants. He also had a garden in Taa·if called al-Waht that was worth a thousand thousand (1,000,000) dirhams.

The people of Egypt took a great deal of knowledge from him.

He passed away in Egypt in the year 65 H, during the nights of the siege of the capital -al-Fustaat- so when he died they were not able to take his funeral out because of the war between Marwaan ibn al-Hakam and the army of Ibn az-Zubayr. So he was buried in his home *-radiyallaahu `anhu.* Those who narrated from him included Ibn al-Musayyib, `Ikrimah, Aboo `Abdir-Rahmaan al-Hubulee, `Urwah, Wahb, Ibn Abee Mulaykah, and Aboo `Amr Shu`ayb ibn Muhammad his grandson.

Those who narrated from him were: his son Muhammad - even though there is dispute about this, and narrations of Muhammad from him are reported in Aboo Daawood, at-Tirmidhee and an-Nasaa·ee; and his freed-slave Aboo Qaaboos, and his grandson Shu`ayb ibn Muhammad - who reported a great deal from him; and he served him and kept his company constantly, and he was brought up in his apartment because Shu`ayb's father Muhammad died in the life time of his father `Abdullaah.

His students were many and included: his freed-slave Ismaa`eel, and his freed-slave Saalim, and Anas ibn Maalik, Aboo Umaamah ibn Sahl, and Jubayr ibn Nufayr; and Sa`eed ibn al-Musayyib, `Urwah, Aboo Salamah ibn `Abdir-Rahmaan, Zirr ibn Hubaysh, Humayd ibn `Abdir-Rahmaan ibn `Awf, Khaythamah ibn `Abdir-Rahmaan al-Ju`fee, Taawoos, ash-Sha`bee, `Ikrimah, `Ataa·, Mujaahid, al-Hasan al-Basree, `Abdullaah ibn Buraydah, Ibn Abee Mulaykah, `Abdur-Rahmaan ibn Jubayr, `Ataa· ibn Yasaar, `Uqbah ibn Muslim, `Amr ibn Deenaar, Masrooq ibn al-Ajda`, Aboo Burdah ibn Abee Moosaa.

Qataadah said: "He was a stout man."

Hammaad ibn Salamah narrated: from `Alee ibn Zayd [[ibn Jud`aan]]: from al-`Uryaan ibn al-Haytham who said: "I came in a deputation along with my father to Yazeed. So a very tall man came. He was reddish and had a large belly. So he sat down. I said: 'Who is this?' So it was said: `Abdullaah ibn `Amr."…

Yahyaa ibn Ayyoob narrated: from Aboo Qabeel: from `Abdullaah ibn `Amr that he said: "We used to write down what Allaah's Messenger (ﷺ) said in his presence."..

[[…Yoosuf ibn Maahak: from `Abdullaah ibn `Amr who said: I used to write down everything which I heard from Allaah's Messenger (ﷺ), wanting to memorize it. So the Quraish forbade me and said: 'Do you write everything when Allaah's Messenger (ﷺ) is a man, and speaks when angry and when pleased!' So I stopped writing, and then mentioned it to Allaah's Messenger (ﷺ), so he indicated with his finger to his mouth and said: << Write, for by the One in Whose Hand is my soul, nothing comes out of it except what is true. >> (Saheeh: as-Saheehah: no. 1532)]]

It is established from `Amr ibn Deenaar: from Wahb ibn Munabbih: from his brother Hammaam that he heard Aboo Hurairah say: "No Companion of Allaah's Messenger (ﷺ) had more ahaadeeth than me, except for `Abdullaah ibn `Amr, because he used to write and I do not write."…

Qutaybah narrated: al-Layth narrated to us, along with someone else: from `Ayyaash ibn `Abbaas: from Aboo `Abdir-Rahmaan al-Hubulee: I heard `Abdullaah ibn `Amr say: "That I should be the tenth of ten poor people on the Day of Resurrection is more beloved to me than that I should be the tenth of ten wealthy people; for those with most will be the ones with the least on the Day of Resurrection, except for those who do like this and like this: meaning: they give in charity to the right and to the left."

[[al-Bukhaaree narrated in his 'Saheeh' (no. 5052): Moosaa narrated to us: Aboo `Awaanah narrated to us: from Mugheerah: from Mujaahid: from `Abdullaah ibn `Amr who said: "My father got me married to a woman of a noble family, so he often used to ask my wife about me. So she said: 'What a fine man he is, for a man who does not come to my bed, nor has he approached me since he married me.' So when that continued for a long time he mentioned it to the Prophet (ﷺ) who said: << Let me meet him. >> So I met him afterwards and he said: << How do you observe fasting? >> So I replied: "I fast every day." He said: << How long does it take you to complete reading the Qur·aan? >> I said: "I do so every night." He said: << Fast for three days every month and recite the Qur·aan once every month. >> I said: "I have strength to do more than that." He said: << Then fast the most excellent fast: the fast of Daawood: Fasting one day and refraining from fasting the next day; and finish the recitation of the whole Qur·aan once in seven nights. >>

Would that I had accepted the concession of Allaah's Messenger (ﷺ), as I have become a weak old man."
So he used to recite one seventh of the Qur·aan to some of his family during the day to make sure that he remembered it for the night; and whenever he wanted to gain some strength he would abstain from fasting for some days, count them and fast them later on for he disliked leaving something which he used to do during the time of the Prophet (ﷺ)]]

I [i.e. adh-Dhahabee] say: He inherited a very great deal of Egyptian gold from his father, so he was one of the kings amongst the Companions.
…`Abdullaah accepted Islaam, and migrated after the seventh year and took part in some of the battles.

Aboo `Ubayd said: "He was in command of the right flank of the army of Mu`aawiyah on the day of Siffeen."

Khaleefah ibn Khayyaat mentions him as one of Mu`aawiyah's governors of Koofah. He said: Then he removed him from that position and replaced him with al-Mugheerah ibn Shu`bah.

There occurs in the 'Musnad' of Ahmad: Yazeed narrated to us: al-`Awwaam related to us: Aswad ibn Mas`ood narrated to me: from Hanzalah ibn Khuwaylid al-`Anbaree who said: "I was in the presence of Mu`aawiyah when two men came to him disputing with regard to the head of `Ammaar -*radiyallaahu `anhu*, so each one of them was saying: 'I killed him.' So `Abdullaah ibn `Amr said: "Each one of you should be pleased that it was his companion who killed him, and not himself, for I heard Allaah's Messenger (ﷺ) say: << The transgressing party will kill him. >> So Mu`aawiyah said: "O `Amr! Will you not spare us this crazy person of yours? Then why are you with us?!" He [i.e. `Abdullaah ibn `Amr] said: "My father made a complaint to Allaah's Messenger (ﷺ), so he said to me: << Obey your father as long as he lives. >> So therefore I am with you, but I will not fight."
[['Saheeh': 'as-Saheehul-Musnad' of Shaikh Muqbil]]

Naafi` ibn `Umar related: from Ibn Abee Mulaykah who said: `Abdullaah ibn `Amr *-radiyallaahu `anhumaa-* said: "What have I to do with Siffeen! What have I to do with fighting against the Muslims! I wish that I had died twenty years - or he said: ten years-before it. Yet even so, by Allaah, I did not strike a sword, nor fire any arrow"; and it is mentioned that he held the flag."

Husayn al-Mu`allim related: from Ibn Buraydah: from Sulaymaan ibn ar-Rabee' al-`Adawee: that he performed Hajj in the time of Mu`aawiyah amongst a group of the reciters: so it was told to us that `Abdullaah [ibn `Amr] is to be found in the lower part of Makkah. So we went towards him and found a very great party of people and baggage, with three hundred camels: one hundred for riding and two hundred for carrying, whereas we used to be told that he was one of the most humble of people. So we said: 'What is all this?' They said: 'It is for his brothers; he conveys them, and whoever stays as a guest with him upon them.' So we were surprised. So they said: He is a wealthy man, and they told us where to find him in the Masjidul-Haraam. So we went to him and found that he was a short man with mucus upon his eye-lids, and he was wearing a simple cloak and waist-wrapper and a turban, and he let his shoes hang at his left side."

...Yahyaa ibn Bukayr said: "`Abdullaah ibn `Amr died in Egypt, and was buried in his small house, in the year 65 H." This saying about the year of his death was also stated by Khaleefah, Aboo `Ubayd, al-Waaqidee, al-Fallaas and others...

MUJAAHID IBN JABR:

"Mujaahid ibn Jabr, the Imaam. Abul-Hajjaaj al-Makhzoomee - their mawlaa (freed-slave), al- Makkee, the reciter, the Mufassir, al-Haafiz. The slave belonging to as-Saa·ib ibn Abis-Saa·ib al-Makhzoomee. He learned from Sa`d, `Aa·ishah, Aboo Hurairah, Umm Haani·, `Abdullaah ibn `Umar, and Ibn `Abbaas and he closely accompanied him for some time, and he learnt the reading of the Qur·aan from him and Tafseer and Fiqh. He was one of the stores of knowledge.

Those who narrated from him included `Ikrimah, Taawoos, and `Ataa· - and they were his contemporaries; and `Amr ibn Deenar, Abuz-Zubayr, al-Hakam ibn `Utaybah, Ibn Abee Najeeh, Mansoor ibn al-Mu`tamir,

Sulaymaan ibn A`mash, Ayyoob as-Sakhtiyaanee, Ibn `Awn, `Umar ibn Dharr, Ma`roof ibn Mushkaan, Qataadah ibn Di`aamah, al-Fadl ibn Maymoon, Ibraaheem ibn Muhaajir, Humayd al-A`raj, Bukayr ibn al-Akhnas, al-Hasan al-Fuqaymee, Khusayf, Sulaymaan al-Ahwal, Sayf ibn Sulaymaan, `Abdul-Kareem al-Jazaree, Aboo Haseen, al-`Awwaam ibn Hawshab, Fitr ibn Khaleefah, an-Nadr ibn `Arabee, and many others.
A group learned the recitation from him, including Ibn Katheer ad-Daaree, Aboo `Amr ibn al-`Alaa·, and Ibn Muhaysin.

Mujaahid said: "I read the entire Qur·aan to Ibn `Abbaas three times, stopping at each Aayah and asking what it was sent down concerning and how it was."
Qataadah said: "The most knowledgeable one remaining with regard to tafseer is Mujaahid."

Ibn Juraij said: "To have learned from Mujaahid would have been more beloved to me than my family and my wealth."

Khusayf said: "The most knowledgeable of them concerning tafseer is Mujaahid."

Sufyaan ath-Thawree said: "Take Tafseer from four: Mujaahid, Sa`eed ibn Jubayr, `Ikrimah, and ad-Dahhaak."

adh-Dhahabee said: It is said that he settled in Koofah at the end of his life, and he used to frequently travel and move about.

al-A`mash said: "When I used to see Mujaahid I would think little of him; he would be wearing worn-out clothing, as if he were a mule-driver who had lost his donkey and was concerned about it; but when he spoke, pearls [[of wisdom]] came out from his mouth."

...A number of people said: he died in the year 103 H.
al-Waaqidee narrated from Ibn Jurayj that he said: "He reached the age of eighty three."..."

Ya`laa ibn `Ubayd: from al-A`mash: from Mujaahid that he said: "I do not know which of the two favours is greater: that He guided me to Islaam, or that He saved me from these innovated sects." [adh-Dhahabee said: Such as those of the Raafidah, the Qadariyyah, and the Jahmiyyah."]

Yahyaa ibn Sulaym said: `Abdul-Wahhaab ibn Mujaahid narrated to us, saying: I was with my father when his son Ya`qoob came and said: 'O my father, we have companions who claim that Eemaan of the inhabitants of the heavens and the inhabitants of the earth is one (and the same.) So he said: "O my son, those people are not my companions. Allaah does not make a person who is drowned in sins just like a person who has no sin."

Aboo Nu`aym said: Mujaahid died whilst prostrating in the year 102 H...
Ibn Hibbaan said: "He died in Makkah in the year 102 or 103 H in prostration having been born in the year 21 H in the Khilaafah of `Umar."

Sufyaan ath-Thawree said: "If tafseer comes to you from Mujaahid then that is enough for you." Therefore his tafseer was relied upon by ash-Shaafi`ee, al-Bukhaaree and others from the people of knowledge, and likewise by Imaam Ahmad and others who complied works of tafseer: they repeatedly bring chains of narration from Mujaahid; more often than from anyone besides him.

['Tahdheebut-Tahdheeb', 'Majmoo`ul-Fataawaa' (13/332), 'Siyar A`laamin-Nubalaa·' (4/449-457), 'Tadhkiratul-Huffaaz' (1/92)]]

QATAADAH IBN DI`AAMAH IBN QATAADAH AS-SADOOSEE:

Qataadah ibn Di`aamah ibn Qataadah ibn `Azeez, al-Haafiz, al-`Allaamah, Abul-Khattaab, as-Sadoosee, al-Basree. He was blind, having been born blind. The Mufassir. He narrated from Anas ibn Maalik and Abut-Tufayl al-Laythee *-radiyallaahu `anhumaa*, and from: Sa`eed ibn al-Musayyib, `Ikrimah, Abush-Sha`thaa· Jaabir ibn Zayd, al-Hasan al-Basree, Muhammad ibn Seereen, `Ataa· ibn Abee Rabaah, Aboo `Uthmaan an-Nahdee, Aboo Buraydah ibn Abee Moosaa, ash-Sha`bee, `Abdullaah ibn Shaqeeq, Mutarrif ibn ash-Shikhkheer, Hafsah bint Seereen, and others.

His students included: Mis`ar ibn Kidaam, Sa`eed ibn Abee `Aroobah, Hammaad ibn Salamah, Ayyoob as-Sakhtiyaanee, Sulaymaan at-Taymee, Shu`bah, Ma`mar, al-Awzaa`ee, al-Layth ibn Sa`d, and others. Yahyaa ibn Ma`een said: "Qataadah was born in 60 H, and he was from Sadoos."

Ma`mar from Qataadah: that he stayed with Sa`eed ibn al-Musayyib for eight nights, and on the eighth day he said to him: "Travel on from us, O blind one, for you have completely drained me (of knowledge)."
Sa`eed ibn al-Musayyib said: "No person of `Iraaq has come to me who is better than Qataadah."

Qataadah said: "I never said to a narrator of hadeeth: 'Repeat it to me and my ears never heard anything except that my heart preserved it."

Ibn Seereen said: "Qataadah is the best memorizer amongst the people."

Ma`mar said: Qataadah said: "I sat with al-Hasan (al-Basree) for twelve years. I prayed the Dawn Prayer with him for three years..."

Ma`mar said: I heard Qataadah say: "There is not an Aayah in the Qur·aan except that I have heard something about it."

Ahmad ibn Hanbal said: "Qataadah was a scholar of Tafseer and of the disagreements of the scholars", and he described him with memorization, knowledge of Fiqh, and he praised him highly, and said: "You will rarely find anyone who can take precedence over him."

Aboo Hilaal said: I asked Qataadah about a matter, and he said "I do not know." So I said: 'Say something about it from your opinion." He said: "I have not spoken based upon opinion for forty years"; and at that time he was about fifty years old.

Hammaam said: I heard Qataadah say: "I have not given a verdict based upon opinion for twenty years."

Sufyaan ath-Thawree said: "Was there anyone in the world like Qataadah?!"

Ma`mar said: I said to az-Zuhree: 'In your view was Qataadah the most knowledgeable, or Makhool? He said: 'Rather Qataadah.'

Ahmad ibn Hanbal said: "Qataadah was the best memorizer amongst the people of Basrah. He did not hear anything except that he memorized it."
adh-Dhahabee said: "Along with his memorization, and his knowledge of hadeeth Qataadah was a chief in Arabic and the language, and the history of the Arabs, and lineage."
Aboo `Awaanah said: "I witnessed Qataadah teaching the Qur·aan in Ramadaan."
Sallaam ibn Abee Mutee` said: "Qataadah used to complete the reading of the whole Qur·aan in seven days. Then when Ramadaan came he would complete it in every three. Then when the last ten came he would complete it every night."

Matar al-Warraaq said: Qataadah continued as a student until he died."

adh-Dhahabee said: "They mention narrations of Qataadah, from a group of people, which he did not hear (directly); and he was a 'mudallis'."

Shu`bah said: "When something which he had heard came, Qataadah would say: 'Narrated to us..', and if that which he had not heard came he would say: 'So and so said..'."

Aboo Zur`ah said: "Qataadah was one of the most knowledgeable students of al-Hasan."

Aboo Haatim said: "The most reliable students of Anas were az-Zuhree, and then Qataadah."

Aboo Haatim said: "He died in Waasit during the plague, at the age of fifty six or fifty seven. Seven years after al-Hasan."

Yahyaa ibn Sa`eed said: "He died in the year 117 or 118 H."

[Siyar A`laamin-Nubalaa·' (5/269-283), 'Tahdheebut-Tahdheeb', 'Tadhkiratul-Huffaaz' (1/122-123).

AL-HASAN IBN ABIL HASAN AL-BASREE:

"al-Hasan ibn Abil-Hasan Yasaar:
The Imaam, Shaikhul-Islaam, Aboo Sa`eed al-Basree. It is said that he used to be a mawlaa (slave) belonging to Zayd ibn Thaabit, and it is said: a slave belonging to Jameel ibn Qutbah.
His mother was Khayrah, the slave-girl of Umm Salamah.
He grew up in al-Madeenah; and memorized the Qur·aan in the Khilaafah of `Uthmaan, and heard him give the Khutbah many times.
On the day of the killing of `Uthmaan he was fourteen years old.

Then he grew older and was constant upon Jihaad, and constant upon knowledge and action. He was one of the courageous folk who were mentioned for that...

In the rule of Mu`aawiyah he was a scribe for the governor of Khuraasaan - ar-Rabee` ibn Ziyaad.

He narrated from `Uthmaan, `Imraan ibn Husayn, al-Mugheerah ibn Shu`bah, `Abdur-Rahmaan ibn Samurah, Samurah ibn Jundub, Jundub al-Bajalee, Ibn `Abbaas, Ibn `Umar, Aboo Bakrah, `Amr ibn Taghlib, Jaabir, and many others.

Those who narrated from him include: Qataadah, Ayyoob (as-Sakhtiyaanee), Ibn `Awn, Yoonus (ibn `Ubayd), Khaalid al-Hadhdhaa·, Hishaam ibn Hassaan, Humayd at-Taweel, Jareer ibn Haazim, Shaybaan an-Nahawee, Yazeed ibn Ibraaheem at-Tusturee, Mubaarak ibn Fadaalah, ar-Rabee` ibn Sabeeh, Abaan ibn Yazeed al-`Attars, Qurrah ibn Khaalid, and many others besides them.

Ibn Sa`d said: "He was a comprehensive scholar, lofty, reliable a proof, trustworthy, a worshipper, one who performed frequent acts of worship and sacrifice. He was abundant in knowledge; spoke eloquently, and was handsome"..., until he said: "He is not a proof in those narrations which he narrated in 'mursal' form, and he was a 'mudallis'. So when he says 'From..' with regard to those he did not meet, then he is not taken as proof." He sometimes performed 'tadlees' from those he had met, omitting the intermediary between himself and them, and Allaah knows best.

However he was a great memorizer, a great scholar; from the oceans of knowledge; a jurist concerning the soul; of tremendous status; having no equal. His reminders were beautiful. His admonitions were eloquent and penetrating. He was a chief in the various types of good; and I have written a biography for him in a single volume which I have entitled 'az-Zukhruful-Qasriyy'.
He died in the year 110 H at the age of 88 *-rahimahullaahu ta`aalaa.*"
['Tadhkiratul-Huffaaz': (1/71-72)].

His father Yasaar was a slave taken captive in Maysaan [North of Basrah, in Southern Iraaq]. He settled in al-Madeenah, and was set free, and married. al-Hasan was born two years before the end of the Khilaafah of `Umar and he grew up in Waadee al-Quraa.

adh-Dhahabee said: "He was the noblest of the people of his time, in knowledge and action."

Mu`tamir ibn Sulaymaan said: My father used to say: "al-Hasan is the Shaikh of the people of Basrah."

He learned the recitation of the Qur·aan from Hittaan ibn `Abdillaah ar-Raqaashee.

adh-Dhahabee said: "He was a man who was of perfect build. His form was fine, and he was handsome; and he was described as being one of those who were courageous."

Aboo Burdah said: "I did not see anyone who more closely resembled the Companions of Muhammad (ﷺ) than him."

Humayd ibn Hilaal said: Aboo Qataadah said to us: "Adhere to this Shaikh, for I have not seen anyone closer in opinion to `Umar than him - meaning al-Hasan."

Jurthoomah said: "I saw al-Hasan dyeing his beard yellow every Jumu`ah."

Qataadah said: "I never compared the knowledge of al-Hasan to that of anyone from the scholars except that I found him having superiority over him; except that if anything was problematic for him he would write to Sa`eed ibn al-Musayyib, asking him about it; and I never sat with a jurist except that I saw the superiority of al-Hasan."

Humayd and Yoonus said: "We did not see anyone more perfect in behavior than al-Hasan."

Yoonus ibn `Ubayd said: "I have not seen anyone whose speech more closely matches his actions than al-Hasan."

ar-Rabee` ibn Anas said: "I used to go to al-Hasan for ten years, or as Allaah wished, and there was not a single day except that I would hear from him something which I had not heard before."

Hawshab narrated from al-Hasan that he said:
"O son of Aadam! By Allaah! If you recite the Qur·aan and then truly believe in it, then your grief in this world will be lengthened, your fear in this world will become severe, and your weeping in this world will be plentiful."
['Siyar A`laamin-Nubalaa·' (4/563-588)]

Zaa·idah ibn Qudaamah: from Hishaam ibn Hassaan: al-Hasan said: "When a man used to seek knowledge, then (its effect) would soon be seen upon what he looked at, upon his humility and submission, upon his tongue, upon his ties of kinship, and upon his avoidance of the unnecessary things of the world (*zuhd*)." He said: "And al-Hasan used to say: "Do not sit with the people of the innovated sects (Ahwaa·); do not debate with them; and do not listen to anything from them."
['Tahdheebul-Kamaal']

SUFYAAN IBN SA`EED IBN MASROOQ, ATH-THAWREE:

"Sufyaan ibn Sa`eed ibn Masrooq, the Imaam, Shaikhul-Islaam, The chief of the memorizers, Aboo `Abdillaah, ath-Thawree: from Thawr of the tribe of Mudar, not Thawr of Hamadaan; al-Koofee, the Jurist (Faqeeh).

He narrated from his father, and from: Zubayd ibn al-Haarith, Habeeb ibn Abee Thaabit, al-Aswad ibn Qays, Ziyaad ibn `Ilaaqah, Muhaarib ibn Dithaar, and their level.

Those who narrated from him included: Ibn al-Mubaarak, Yahyaa al-Qattaan, Ibn Wahb, Wakee`, al-Firyaabee, Qabeesah, Aboo Nu`aym, Muhammad ibn Katheer, Ahmad ibn Yoonus al-Yarboo`ee, and very many others.
Shu`bah, Yahyaa ibn Ma`een, and a group said: Sufyaan is the Chief of the Believers in Hadeeth."

Ibn al-Mubaarak said: I wrote (narrations) from one thousand one hundred Shaikhs, and there was not amongst them anyone more excellent than Sufyaan."

Shu`bah used to say: "Sufyaan is a better memorizer than me."

Warqaa· said: "ath-Thawree did not see the like of himself."

Ahmad said: "No one takes precedence over him in my heart."

al-Qattaan said: "I have never seen a better memorizer then him: if you asked him about a question or about a hadeeth which he did not possess, it would trouble him greatly."

`Abdur-Razzaaq said: Sufyaan said: "I never stored anything in my heart and then found it letting me down."

al-Awzaa`ee said: "No one whom the Ummah is united upon in their being pleased with him and holding him to be correct remains except for Sufyaan."

Ibn al-Mubaarak said: "I do not know anyone upon the face of the earth who is more knowledgeable than Sufyaan."

Wakee` said: "Sufyaan was an ocean."

al-Qattaan said: "Sufyaan is above Maalik in everything."

Aboo Usaamah said: "Whoever informs you that he has seen the like of Sufyaan, then do not believe him."

Ibn Abee Dhi·b said: "I have not seen in Iraaq anyone who resembles your Thawree."

ath-Thawree said: "I would love that I am saved regarding knowledge: so that it is neither for nor against me; and there is no action which I fear more for myself than it - meaning Hadeeth."

Yahyaa ibn Yamaan said: I heard Sufyaan say: "The scholar is the doctor of the Religion and dirhams are the disease for the Religion. So if the doctor catches the disease, then when will he be able to treat others?!"

al-Khuraybee said: "I heard ath-Thawree say: "Seeking Hadeeth (itself) is not a preparation for death, rather it is an ailment which a man prescribes himself with."

I (i.e. adh-Dhahabee) say: 'He has spoken the truth, by Allaah. Seeking Hadeeth is something other than Hadeeth itself. So seeking Hadeeth is a term commonly used to cover a number of affairs which are additional to actually acquiring Hadeeth itself, and many of them are just steps towards knowledge; and most of these are affairs which the narrator of hadeeth becomes engrossed with, such as: acquiring fine manuscripts; seeking shorter chains; increasing the number of one's Shaikhs; being overjoyed at titles and praise; and hoping for a long life so that he can narrate more; and loving to be alone in narrating something; and many affairs which are closely allied to personal goals, and not to actions for the Lord. So if your seeking the Prophetic Hadeeth is surrounded by these calamities, then when will you escape from them towards acting purely and sincerely for Allaah. Then if the knowledge of narrations can be tainted, then what do you think about the knowledge of logic, controversial debating, philosophy of the earlier peoples; which strip away Eemaan and produce doubts and throw a person into confusion. These were not, by Allaah, from the knowledge of the Companions, nor the Taabi`een, nor from the knowledge of al-Awzaa`ee, ath-Thawree, Maalik, Aboo Haneefah, Ibn Abee Dhi·b, or Shu`bah; nor, by Allaah, were they known by Ibn al-Mubaarak; nor by Aboo Yoosuf who said: "Whoever seeks the Religion through rhetorical

theology (al-kalaam) will become an evil heretic"; nor by Wakee`, Ibn Mahdee, Ibn Wahb, ash-Shaafi`ee, `Affaan, Aboo `Ubayd, Ibn al-Madeenee, Ahmad Aboo Thawr, al-Muzanee, al-Bukhaaree, al-Athram, Muslim, an-Nasaa·ee, Ibn Khuzaymah, Ibn Suraij, Ibn al-Mundhir, and their like.
Rather their knowledge was the Qur·aan, the Hadeeth, Fiqh, Grammar, and the like. Yes Sufyaan also said, in what al-Firyaabee heard from him: "There is no action more excellent than seeking the Hadeeth, as long as the intention is correct regarding it."

He said: And I heard him say: "If we wanted to narrate Hadeeth to you exactly as we heard it, then we would not narrate a single hadeeth to you."

al-Firyaabee said: I heard Sufyaan say: "I entered upon al-Mahdee and I said: "It reached me that Ibn `Umar spent twelve deenars upon his Hajj, and you are involved in what you are involved in." So he became angry and said: 'Do you want me to be as you are?!' So I said: 'If you are not as I am, then at least reduce from what you are doing. "Damurah said: I heard Maalik say: "Iraaq used to wage war upon us with dirhams and garments, and then it waged war upon us with Sufyaan ath-Thawree."

I say: The virtues of this Imaam occur in a volume complied by Ibn al-Jawzee; and I have abridged it and brought a good quantity of that in my 'Taareekh'.

Saalih Jazarah said: "Sufyaan was a greater memorizer and had more hadeeth than Maalik. However Maalik carefully selected the narrators; and Sufyaan was a greater memorizer then Shu`bah. His ahaadeeth amounted to thirty thousand, whereas the ahaadeeth of Shu`bah were about ten thousand.

"Sufyaan was born in the year 97 H. He began seeking Hadeeth whilst he was a youth, since his father was one of the scholars of Koofah. He (Sufyaan) died in Basrah, in hiding from al-Mahdee, since he was one who spoke out with the truth and strongly criticized. He died in Sha`baan in the year 161 H *-radiyallaahu `anhu.*

It is authentic from Ma`daan: from ath-Thawree, regarding His Saying -He the Most High: ﴿وَهُوَ مَعَكُمْ﴾ [*Sooratul-Hadeed (57): 4*] [[Meaning: And He is with you]], so he said: "His knowledge," and this is what is reported from a group of the people of Tafseer.

al-Laalikaa·ee in 'as-Sunnah': al-Mukhallis related to us: Abul-Fadl Shu`ayb ibn Muhammad related to us: `Alee ibn Harb ibn Bassaam related to us: I heard Shu`ayb ibn Harb say: I said to Sufyaan ath-Thawree:
'Tell me a saying about the Sunnah, through which Allaah will benefit me, and when I stand in front of Him and He asks me about it I can say: 'O my Lord! Sufyaan told this to me.' So that I will be saved and you will be taken.' He said: "Write: In the name of Allaah, the Extremely Merciful, the Bestower of Mercy. The Qur·aan is the Speech of Allaah. It is not created. It came from Him, and it will return to Him. Whoever says other than this then he is an Disbeliever; and Eemaan is statement and action and intention, it increases and decreases; and to give precedence to the two Shaikhs [i.e. Aboo Bakr and `Umar]..." until he said: "O Shu`ayb, what you have written will not benefit you until you hold wiping over the leather socks, and until you hold reciting '*Bismillaahir-Rahmaanir-Raheem*' quietly (in the Prayer) to be better than reciting it loudly; and until you have Eemaan in Pre-Decree (al-Qadr); and until you hold praying behind every righteous or sinful (imaam); and that the Jihaad continues until the Day of Resurrection; and having patience under the flag of the ruler, whether he is tyrannical or just." So I said: 'O Aboo `Abdillaah, is that every Prayer?' He said: "No, rather the Jumu`ah Prayer, and the two `Eid Prayers: pray them behind whoever you reach. As for the rest of that, then you have a choice, so do not pray except behind one whom you trust in, and you know that he is from the people of the Sunnah.

If you stand before Allaah and He asks you about this, then say: "O my Lord, Sufyaan ibn Sa`eed related it to me; and then leave me to my Lord - the Mighty and Majestic."

This is established from Sufyaan, and the Shaikh of al-Mukhallis is reliable -may Allaah have mercy upon them.
['Tadhkiratul-Huffaaz' (1/203-207)]

[[For the full narration, and a longer biography of Sufyaan refer to the book 'Mountains of Knowledge.']]

IBRAAHEEM AN-NAKHA`EE:

"Ibraaheem an-Nakha`ee, the Jurist (Faqeeh) of Iraaq. Aboo `Imraan, Ibraaheem ibn Yazeed ibn Qays ibn al-Aswad, al-Koofee, al-Faqeeh.
He narrated from `Alqamah, Masrooq, al-Aswad, and a group.

He entered upon Ummul-Mu·mineen `Aa·ishah *-radiyallaahu `anhaa-* whilst he was a child.

Those who took from him included: Hammaad ibn Sulaymaan - the jurist, Sammaak ibn Harb, al-Hakam ibn `Utaybah, Ibn `Awn, al-A`mash, Mansoor, and many others.

He was one of the scholars possessing Ikhlaas (making ones intentions and actions purely and sincerely for Allaah).

Mugheerah said: "We used to have awe for Ibraaheem just as we had awe of the ruler."

al-A`mash said: "I would sometimes see Ibraaheem praying, and then he would come to us and remain for a while, as if he was a person who was ill"; and he said: "Ibraaheem was a skillful verifier in hadeeth, and he used to be on his guard against fame, and he would not sit against a pillar."

When ash-Sha`bee heard of the death of Ibraaheem he said: "He has not left anyone behind who is like him."

Ibn `Awn said: "Ibraaheem used to go to the rulers and request gifts."

al-Hasan ibn `Amr al-Fuqaymee said: "Ibraaheem used to buy a goose, fatten it up, and give it as a gift to the rulers."

Aboo Haneefah related from Hammaad who said: "I gave the good news of the death of al-Hajjaaj to Ibraaheem. So he prostrated and wept out of joy."

`Abdul-Malik ibn Abee Sulaymaan said: "I heard Sa`eed ibn Jubayr say: "You ask me for verdicts when you have amongst you Ibraaheem an-Nakha`ee?!"

Hunaydah, the wife of Ibraaheem, said that he used to fast one day and refrain from fasting for one day; and it is reported through a number of chains from Ibraaheem that he would not speak regarding knowledge unless he was asked.

Ibn `Awn reported from Ibraaheem that he said: "They used to hate, when they gathered together, that a man should display the best of what he had."

Ibraaheem died at the end of the year 95 H, in middle age, before entering old age -*rahimahullaah ta`aalaa.*
['Tadhkiratul-Huffaaz': 1/73-74]

The Imaam, the Haafiz, the Jurist of Iraaq;...
Al-Yamaanee, then al-Koofee, one of the great scholars.

He was the son of Mulaykah - the sister of al-Aswad ibn Yazeed.

He narrated from his maternal uncle [i.e. al-Aswad], and from Masrooq, `Alqamah ibn Qays, `Abeedah as-Salmaanee, Aboo Zur`ah al-Bajalee, Khaythamah ibn `Abdir-Rahmaan, ar-Rabee` ibn Khuthaym, Abush-Sha`thaa· al-Muhaaribee, Sahm ibn Minjaab, Suwayd ibn Ghafalah, al-Qaadee Shurayh, Shurayh ibn Artaat, Aboo Ma`mar `Abdullaah ibn Sakhbarah, `Ubayd ibn Nudaylah, `Umaarah ibn `Umayr, Aboo `Ubaydah ibn `Abdillaah, Aboo `Abdir-Rahmaan as-Sulamee, his maternal uncle `Abdur-Rahmaan ibn Yazeed, Hammaam ibn al-Haarith, and many others from the major Taabi`een...

He was the Muftee for the people of Koofah, along with ash-Sha`bee, in their time; and he was a righteous man, a jurist, cautious against sin, little in whatever was unnecessary, and he was in hiding from al-Hajjaaj.

Ibn `Awn said: I described Ibraaheem to Ibn Seereen, so he said: "Perhaps he was that weak-eyed youth who used to sit along with us in the presence of `Alqamah. He was amongst the people, but it was as if he was not from them."
Shu`bah: from Mansoor: from Ibraaheem who said: "I have never written anything down."

al-Haakim said: Ibraaheem an-Nakha`ee used to perform the Hajj along with his paternal uncle and his maternal uncle: `Alqamah and al-Aswad, and he used to hate the Murji·ah, and say: I fear more for this Ummah from the Murji·ah than from a like number of the Azaariqah [i.e. the Khawaarij]."

He died at the age of forty nine.

Shu`ayb ibn al-Habhaab said: I was one of those who buried Ibraaheem an-Nakha`ee at night, and we were seven or nine in number. So ash-Sha`bee said: "Have you buried your companion?" I said: 'Yes.' He said: "He has not left behind anyone more knowledgeable than himself, or having greater Fiqh than him." I said: 'Not even al-Hasan, and not even Ibn Seereen?' He said: "Yes, not even from the people of Basrah, nor from the people of Koofah, nor from the people of the Hijaaz- and in one narration: nor from the people of Shaam." With regard to the age of Ibraaheem, then there are two sayings: one of them is that he lived for forty nine years; the second is that he lived for fifty eight years. He died in the year 96 H.

Ahmad ibn Hanbal said: "Ibraaheem was a person of intelligence, a memorizer, a person of Sunnah."

Mugheerah said: If a person whom Ibraaheem did not wish to meet came looking for him his slave-girl would go out and say: "Seek him in the mosque."

Aboo `Amr ad-Daanee said: Ibraaheem learnt the recitation from `Alqamah and al-Aswad. al-A`mash and Talhah ibn Musarrif learned the recitation from him."

Wakee` narrated from Shu`bah: from Mugheerah from Ibraaheem who said: "Reciting '*Bismillaahir-Rahmaanir-Raheem*' (in the Prayer) loudly is an innovation."

[Siyar A`laamin-Nubalaa·' (4/520-529)]

“MAS`OOD IBN MAALIK, ABOO RAZEEN, al-Asadee; of Koofah.

Fully reliable and distinguished; from the second level [the elder taabi`een]. He died in the year 85 H…” [‘Taqreebut-Tahdheeb’]
He narrated from Mu`aadh ibn Jabal, `Alee ibn Abee Taalib, Aboo Moosaa al-Ash`aree, Aboo Hurairah, Ibn `Abbaas and others from the Companions - *radiyallaahu `anhum.*

“`ABDUR-RAHMAAN IBN ZAYD IBN ASLAM:

al-`Adawee, al-Madanee, the mawlaa (freed slave) of `Umar ibn al-Khattaab.

Declared weak in narrating hadeeth by Ahmad, Ibn al-Madeenee, an-Nasaa·ee and others.” [‘Tahdheebul-Kamaal’]

adh-Dhahabee said in Siyar A`laamin-Nubalaa·’ (8/349):
“`Abdur-Rahmaan was a champion of the Qur·aan and Tafseer. He gathered a Tafseer in a single volume, and a book of the Abrogating and the Abrogated…
He died in the year 182 H.”

Shaikhul-Islaam Ibn Taimiyyah said: “He was an imaam, and he took the Tafseer from his father; and Zayd was an imaam concerning it, and Maalik and others accepted the Tafseer from him; and `Abdullaah ibn Wahb, the companion of Maalik, took it from him, and Asbigh ibn al-Faraj, the jurist.” [‘Majmoo`ul-Fataawaa’ (15/67-68).]

“`ALEE IBN ABEE TALHAH - SAALIM:

The mawlaa of Banul-`Abbaas. He lived in Hims. He related things by way of ‘irsaal’ from Ibn `Abbaas but did not see him. From the sixth level [those who lived amongst the later taabi`een, but it is not established that they met

any Companions. He was generally acceptable (sadooq) but made some errors in narrating. He died in the year 143 H." ['Taqreebut-Tahdheeb']
Ibn Hajr said: "He did not hear from Ibn `Abbaas, rather between them was Mujaahid," and he said: "al-Bukhaaree quoted a great deal from his tafseer, from the narration of Mu`aawiyah ibn Saalih from him: from Ibn `Abbaas in the chapter headings and elsewhere, but he would not name him, saying rather: 'Ibn `Abbaas said...', or 'It is mentioned from Ibn `Abbaas..." ['Tahdheebut-Tahdheeb']

Aboo Ja`far an-Nahhaas narrated that Imaam Ahmad said: "There is in Egypt the manuscript of a tafseer which `Alee ibn Abee Talhah narrates. If a person were to travel to Egypt just for that it would not be too much." ['an-Naasikh wal-Mansookh' of an-Nahhaas (p. 16).]

Yoosuf ibn `Abdul-Hadee al-Hanbalee said: "Many tafseers have been related from Ibn `Abbaas for the entire Qur·aan, with many different chains of narration, and from the finest of them is that reported by Mu`aawiyah ibn Saalih: from `Alee ibn Abee Talhah: from Ibn `Abbaas." Then he mentioned the disconnection in its chain of narration, and mentioned that the missing connection is Mujaahid, and also `Ikrimah.
['Hidaayatul-Insaan ilal istighnaa· bil-Qur·aan', quoted in 'at-Tafseerus-Saheeh'(1/48).]

as-Suyootee related from Ibn Hajr that he said: "When the missing link is known, and found to be reliable, then there is no harm in that" ['al-Itqaan'].

TRANSLATOR'S REFERENCES:

- *Adwaa·ul-Bayaan fee eedaahil-Qur·aan bil-Qur·aan*. Muhammad al-Ameen ash-Shanqeetee; and its completion by Shaikh `Atiyyah Muhammad Saalim. `Aalamul-Kutub, Beirut.

- *al-`Ujaab fee bayaanil-Asbaab*. Ahmad ibn `Alee ibn Muhammad ibn Hajr. Daar Ibn Hazm, Beirut, 1422 H.

- *al-`Uqoodud-Durriyyah fee manaaqib Shaikhil-Islaam Ahmad ibn Taimiyyah*. Muhammad ibn Ahmad ibn `Abdil-Haadee. Verified by Muhammad Haamid al-Faqqee. Daar al-Kitaab al-`Arabee, Beirut.

- *al-Baa`ithul-Hatheeth Sharh Ikhtisaar `Uloomil-Hadeeth*. Ismaa`eel ibn Katheer. Daarul-`Aasimah, Riyadh, 1415 H.

- *al-Badrut-Taali`*. Muhammad ibn `Alee ash-Shawkaanee. Daarul-kutubil-`ilmiyyah, Beirut, 1418 H.

- *al-Bidaayah wan-Nihaayah*. Ismaa`eel ibn Katheer. Daarul-Kutubil-`Ilmiyyah, Beirut, 4th edn., 1408 H.

- *al-Jaami`us-Saheeh*. Muhammad ibn Ismaa`eel al-Bukhaaree. Daar Tawqin-Najaat, Beirut, 1422 H.

- *al-Kaashif*. adh-Dhahabee, Muhammad ibn Ahmad. Daarul-Kutubil-`Ilmiyyah, Beirut, 1403 H.

- *al-Mu`jamul-Kabeer*. Sulaymaan ibn Ahmad at-Tabaraanee; verified by Hamdee `Abdul-Majeed as-Salafee. Maktabah Ibn Taimiyyah, Cairo.

- *al-Musnad*. Ahmad ibn Muhammad ibn Hanbal; verified by Shu`ayb al-Arnawoot. Mu·assasatur-Risaalah, Beirut, 2nd edn., 1420 H.

- *al-Muwatta·*. Maalik ibn Anas; verified by Fu·aad `Abdil-Baaqee. Daar Ihyaa·il-Kutubil-`Arabiyyah.

-*an-Naasikh wal-Mansookh*; an-Nahhaas,Muhammad ibn Ahmad. Mu·assasatul-kutubith-thiqaafiyyah, Beirut, 2nd edn.

- *Arabic-English Lexicon.* E.W.Lane, The Islamic Texts Society, Cambridge, reprinted 1984, (first printed 1863).

- *as-Saheehul-Musnad min Dalaa·ilin-Nubuwwah.* Muqbil ibn Haadee al-Waadi`ee. Daarul-Arqam, Kuwait, 1405 H.

- *as-Saheehul-Musnad min Fadaa·ilis-Sahaabah.* Mustafaa al-`Adawee. Daar Ibn `Affaan, al-Khobar, 2nd edn. 1419 H.

- *at-Taajul-Mukallal.* Siddeeq Hasan Khaan. Maktabah Daaris-Salaam, Riyadh, 1416 H.

- *at-Tafseerus-Saheeh mawsoo`atas-saheehil-masboor minat-tafseer bil-ma·thoor.* Hikmat ibn Basheer Yaaseen. Daarul-Ma·aathir, al-Madeenah, 1419 H.

- *Badaa·i`ut-tafseer al-jaami` li tafseeril-Imaam ibn Qayyimil-Jawziyyah.* Compiled by Yusree as-Sayyid Muhammad. Daar Ibn al-Jawzee, Dammaam, 1414 H.

- *A Dictionary and Glossary of the Koran.* John Penrice. Curzon Press, London, (1873) , new edn. (reprinted) 1979.

- *Fathul-Baaree Sharh Saheehil-Bukhaaree.* Ahmad ibn `Alee al-`Asqalaanee. Daarul-Ma`rifah, Beirut.

- *Fathul-Qadeer bayna fanayyir-riwaayah wad-diraayah min `ilmit-tafseer.* Muhammad ibn `Alee ash-Shawkaanee. Daar Ihyaa·it-Turaathil-`Arabee, Beirut.

- *Interpretation of the Meanings of the Noble Qur·aan.* Taqi-ud-Din Al-Hilali and Muhammad Muhsin Khan. Darussalam, Riyadh, 1996.

- *Taqreebut-Tahdheeb.* Ahmad ibn `Alee al-`Asqalaanee; verified by Abul-Ashbaal Sagheer Ahmad Shaaghif. Daarul-`Aasimah, Riyadh, 1416 H.

- *Tayseerul-Kareemir-Rahmaan fee Tafseer Kalamil-Mannaan.* `Abdur-Rahmaan ibn Naasir as-Sa`dee. Mu·assasatur-Risaalah, Beirut, 1421 H.

- *The Qur·an, Arabic Text with corresponding English meanings.* Saheeh International. Abul-Qaasim Publishing House, Jeddah, 1997.

- *The translation of the meanings of Sahih al-Bukhari.* Muhammad Muhsin Khan. Darussalam, Riyadh, 1997.

- *Zaadul-Maseer fee `ilmit-tafseer.* `Abdur-Rahmaan ibn `Alee ibn Muhammad ibn al-Jawzee. al-Maktabul-Islaamee, Beirut, Damascus, 4th edn., 1407 H.